Betrayal of Love

Jacqueline Tyecise McDuffie
http://www.wix.com/AuthorJacqueline/Jacqueline-Tyecise-McDuffie

Dedication:

This book is dedicated to my family and friends but, most of all, my parents and children.

Also by Jacqueline McDuffie:

Dedication:
This book is dedicated to my family and friends but, most of all, my parents and children.

A Diamond in the Rough

Betrayal of Love

ISBN-13:
978-0615488929
(JackieUrbanExpressionsPublishing)

ISBN-10:
0615488927

This is a work of fiction. All of the characters, names, living or dead, incidents, organizations, and

dialogue in this novel are either products of the author's imagination or are used fictitiously.
Printed in the United States of America
Book Cover Design by Jonathan Johnson
Editing and Interior Design by Brandie Randolph

Warning!

This book contains sexually explicit content and language. It is not recommended for those under age 18.

This novel is raw and uncut- straightforward sex, lies, betrayal. Caution! Beware of juicy drama that will have you on the edge of your seat wanting more and more! Enjoy every chapter of Jocelyn and Bryant Carter's rollercoaster relationship.

I always say, "never judge a book by its cover; don't judge me until you know me!"

Love and Peace,

Ms. Jackie

Acknowledgments

First, I have to give all glory and praise to GOD, my Lord and Savior. Thank you for this opportunity!

My first novel is called A Diamond in the Rough. I've learned to appreciate the small things in life. I appreciate good people-those who believed and supported my movement. What you are expecting is already expecting you. People who I've met encourage me to keep writing. Those who read my first novel, this acknowledgement is for you, too. My family, I love you so deeply.

I truly believe family comes first. I am a provider, writer, mother, and a person with a great sense of humor and heart. I never thought that I would be able to accomplish something big like this. My dream has always been writing; my weakness is not pursuing my dream and, instead, ignoring it. I want to give thanks to all of my supporters. My heart is heavy and as long as I stay humble and continue to work in God's favor; my novels will go a long way.

I have received good advice from my loyal readership. I can only say that I am glad people can relate to these stories. I don't want to be like anybody else but me. A lot of authors inspired me to never give up. When I was younger, I would always read my mom my raps and poems and she would listen to me express my feelings. She was always the type to listen, whether it was good or bad. My sisters and brothers are always in my heart. There's nothing in this world I'd rather do than write. I love every part of it. My kids,Jaquante, Dajanae, and Jerome, I love you so dearly. Prayer really works; I witnessed it and GOD has answered my prayers.

I am a sinner who has been saved by grace. It's by the grace of God that I'm here. We all have sinned and fallen short on God's direction. I ask God to forgive me for my sins. Every day, I ask for a new cleansing.

Confession Time
Chapter 1

If only I would have listened to that voice in my head that kept whispering to me, saying, *Jocelyn, don't do it; don't kill your husband.* I wouldn't be in this predicament right now.

I loved that man so much that I was so blind.

Sometimes, love can hurt, in a good or bad way.

There was nothing in this world that I wouldn't do for that man. I would have died for him and my girls. Bryant was my first and only love. At times, I wanted to kill myself. Bryant and I started dating when we were in high school and had been dating ever since.

Shit, we end up getting married.

I found myself in the same situation, over and over again.

Was this marriage a game to him? How could Bryant cheat on me and hurt me for all those years?

"I invested in this man like I invested in my hair business. Whatever Bryant told me to do, I did it. I loved him so much, but I refuse to let him use me. I got tired of the lies, the cheating, the fighting, and him disrespecting shit, I got fucking fed up. So, yes, I killed my husband. I stabbed his ass 25 times, 10 times in his stomach and 15 times in his heart. I dragged his body toward our bathroom, picked his body up, and put him in our

Jacuzzi tub with sulfuric acid. I watched his body sizzle and watched him decompose quickly".

Tears ran down my face from the fumes that almost had me vomiting. My mind went blank and my heart was racing. Once his body decomposed, I left the bathroom with no remorse. Then, I slammed the door shut!

The detective looked at Jocelyn and asked her to start the story from the beginning on how she met Bryant. Detective Charles Mack pushed the record button and said, "now, remember, I need your statement, word for word, every single detail. This may help you in court for the jury."

Detective Charles Mack took Jocelyn's handcuffs off and offered her a cigarette. Jocelyn took the cigarette and lit it. She took a long puff and said, "Now this could get a little emotional. I need to calm my nerves."

Jocelyn knew she was going to be in jail for a long time. She had been in there a month and it felt like a century. Her girls never understood what had happened. They thought their parents were the perfect couple. They loved both of them unconditionally and the same.

Detective Mack pressed the record button again and stated, "Today, Monday, January 10, 2010 around 7:30am. I am here with inmate Jocelyn Chanel Carter. Please state for the jury, word for word, what happened, but start from when you and Mr. Bryant James Carter met. Please begin."

Jocelyn began with the story.

"The year of 1997 is when I met Bryant James Carter," Jocelyn said. "Now, Bryant was the popular type in high school and everybody loved his sense of humor. He just transfers from another high school because him, his mom, and sister moved into the area. The handsome, pretty boy Casanova was the type to talk any girl's panties off; all the girls loved that baby boyish look with those pretty white teeth, those waves, and goatee he wore."She puffed her cigarette again. "But, little me, I was the conservative type, like my bourgeois mom. I had it going on. I worked at CVS, getting paid at least close to $300 a week and I drove a 1995 silver Lexus that my father bought me for my 16th birthday. I met Bryant in the hallway at my locker and, what a coincidence, his locker was two lockers down. I guess I was his main target. So, he came over there to me and asks to take me to the movies one night. He was so bold. I immediately rejected the offer, rolled my eyes, grabbed my books, slammed my locker, and walked away. Demanding as he was, Bryant grabbed my arm and slipped me one of his business cards inside of my science book and told me to call him later.

I waved my hand up, saying what-ever and switched my petite ass away from him, walking down the hallway. I felt his eyes undressing me he watched me go into my science classroom, and then he walked in the opposite direction.

After school let out, Bryant was over there talking with his boys. He watched me come out of the school building walking toward my car. He stared at me until I drove off."

"That bitch is sneaky; you better watch her. She doesn't conversate with anybody else but her bourgeois ass friends. You better watch out for those quiet ones; they get you every time."

"Crazy ass brauds," Mike said to Bryant, smiling.

"Naw, she's not like them others hoes. She's been hurt before, you can tell, or maybe she's gay, or maybe she listen to her parents all the time."

"If she's gay, that works for me. Two for fun, even better," said Bryant, giving Mike a high five and smiling.

"I may be a little patient. She'll come around, watch and see my work, playboy," said Bryant.

"Whatever, playboy, you not getting those draws, I bet you," said Mike.

"Whatever," said Bryant, as he walked away, heading toward his truck. "I will talk to you niggas later, man."He jumped in his truck and drove off, blasting his Tupac Shakur CD in his booming system.

I drove up in front of our million-dollar house in Virginia. My mom was at the dining room table, texting on her cell phone.

"Hey, Mom, what's good?" I said to her.

"Nothing much, baby girl, reading these text messages about my daily horoscope," said Marilyn. I smile at her.

"Hey, baby," said Steven, as he walked into the dining room area.

"Hey, Dad, what's for dinner? You know I like that steak you be cooking on Tuesday."

Steven walked in the kitchen and said, "I had a hard day at work. You wait until you get our age; you will see how hard it is out here."

"Speak for yourself, Steve, I am way younger than you," said Marilyn. "Don't put that old age on me yet," said Marilyn.

"I love you, too, babe," Steven replied, as he smiled at my mom leaving out of the kitchen and walking upstairs toward the bedroom.

I said to my mom, "I love you. I have to go and get dressed for work. I have to work from 6:00 a.m. until 11:00p.m.tonight. My schedule changed, so now I'm only working four days out of the week, like you requested."I smiled.

"That's right. Remember that big argument me and your dad had because of your school grades? Now, I must admit, your grades have gotten better. But, baby, you are so tired in the morning. That's the only reason I was bitching that time. But, enough about this conversation. I will make sure I tell your father to have your steak ready. I would cook it for you, but Mommy got to stay fit. I don't eat the red meat at all. My figure has to stay looking good for my age. I am only 34. I had you at 17.Must I remind you every day, baby girl?"Marilyn smiled and switched her petite figure upstairs, heading toward the bedroom.

I lived downstairs in the basement where I had it all laid out. I had a brown and cream microfiber love seat and couch with my 42-inch big screen TV mounted on the wall and my computer in the corner where I did most of my studying and networking.

I had a bathroom downstairs and a mini refrigerator. The basement was big that could fit my king-sized waterbed, along with my two nightstands and big wooden dresser.

My parents did not want me to ask a man for shit. I was their only child and all I had to do was graduate and keep my grades up. They really did not want me to move out of their house. I could live off of my parents 'money. They were both worth over a million dollars. That was the total for both of their life insurance policies. I wouldn't have to work again if something were to happen to my parents. The reason I was working for CVS was because I didn't want to depend on them for anything. My dad was the top executive in his law firm and my mother was a real estate agent and broker. She was just sitting on her money and really didn't have to pay for anything.

My dad took care of Marilyn; he used to always call her his black Marilyn Monroe. That's how my dad and she met. He was interested in buying one of her half-million dollar homes in Washington, DC. That house was one of the houses she dreamed of having. She questioned him about his livelihood and asked him if he was married. His response was no and, after they conversed for hours, they fell in love. You know what happened next, of course. It didn't take them long to have me and they moved into the six-bedroom, three-level house a month later.

As I was getting myself dressed, my phone rang. It was my home girl, Saniyah.

"What's up, girl, please tell me you don't have to work tonight. I wanted you to come and hang out at the park with us."

"On a Tuesday? What the hell are y'all getting into?" I replied.

“Nothing, just chilling for a second, then we all are heading home. We have school tomorrow,” said Saniyah.

“Naw, babe, I have to be at work in 40 minutes, so let me get off this phone and get ready to leave out," I said to her. “Y'all be safe and text my phone because you know I can’t answer it at work.”

“I will. I’ll tell the girls you are working tonight,”Saniyah said.

I hung the phone up, opened my French doors, cut the water on, took my clothes off, and got into the steamy hot shower. The steam fogged up the mirrors. It felt so good.

Water ran down my caramel body. I opened my mouth to let the water fill up my mouth. I washed my long, pretty, reddish-brown hair. I almost forgot I had to go to work. I washed my face and body, got out of the shower to dry off, went in my bedroom and closed the door.

I lotioned my body from head to toe. I grabbed my crisp uniform shirt, khaki pants, and fresh New Balance tennis shoes from my walk-in closet and walked upstairs. My keys were on the dining room table, so I grabbed them as I attempted to walk toward the front door.

I can hear my mom moaning out loud. It sounded like a porn movie was playing in the living room. I was getting ready to yell upstairs, but I didn’t want to disturb them having sex, so I proceeded to open the front door. The sensor reminded me about the alarm. I put the code in and then left. I text my mom’s phone that I put the alarm on and I was going to work. My job was 15 minutes away from our house. When I arrived at CVS, I got a parking space right in front of the store. That was our policy- to park closer if we had to work late or close.

Marilyn grabbed her phone while Steven was sexing her from behind, doggy-style. "Babe, got damn, I must not hitting that pussy right. Let me go in real deep in that pussy," Steven whispered in Marilyn's ear.

"No, babe, that's our daughter. She is on her way to work.Ooh, I am sorry, daddy," Marilyn replied, moaning louder and louder. "Yes, daddy, yes," Marilyn moaned. Steven climaxed. They were both tired, so they laid in a fetal position on the bed under the covers, and fell asleep for a quick nap.

It was 10, going on 11, one more hour. *This seems like forever*, I thought. I was now stocking and labeling items on each shelf. My phone vibrated and it was Saniyah. I couldn't read the text because I knew the cameras were watching my every move.

"Hey, Jocelyn, I need your help on the cash register for the remaining hour," said Keith, my sexy manager. That man was fine as hell. He was 6 feet, bald hair, light-skinned and bow-legged with pretty white teeth. I used to have wet dreams about him. I was glad he asked me to get on the register because I knew my time was going to go by fast.

I looked at the time and I had thirty minutes left. I was so glad that I took care of customers, cleaned up my work area, and clocked right out. I ran upstairs to clock out from the time clock. I was watching Keith on the camera. He was so dedicated to his job that he deserved a raise. I knew CVS wasn't paying him much, but he was so nice and very professional at all times.

I walked toward my car and Keith yelled my name."You left your swipe card here," he said. I was embarrassed, so I smiled and walked toward him, grabbed my time card, and said thank you. I was so busy watching him on the camera that I left my time card on the desk next to the time clock.

"See you tomorrow," I said to him, while getting in my car. He waved goodbye and walked back in the store.

I drove off, heading toward my house. I was so tired; I couldn't wait until I hit that comfortable, king-sized bed of mine. I pulled in the garage, got out of my car, clicked the alarm button, and walked in the side door of my basement. I set the alarm, went straight to my bedroom, took my uniform off, and went straight under the covers to go to sleep.

Play No Games
Chapter 2

"Girl, you missed the fun yesterday," said Saniyah.

"I know. I was tired and I have to work again today. I started to not come to school, but nosy Marilyn was home. You know she would have checked on me and asked about 50 questions," I said to her. "Ooh, no, here comes this jerk."

"Girl, who is that? He is fine as hell! If you don't want him, I'll give him some pussy," said Saniyah.

"I don't, so you can have him," I said, giving her a mean look.

"What's up, ladies," Bryant said, as him and Mike walked toward us.

"Nothing, nigga," I said to him, rolling my eyes with my long, curly lashes.

"I am fine, pleased to meet you. And your name is, handsome?" Saniyah said.

"I am Mike and this is Bryant. Mike was a pretty, dark-complexioned boy. He was tall, had white teeth, and wore cornrows all the time. He and Bryant were day and night. When you saw Mike, you saw Bryant. They were stuck on glue together.

I knew they were fucking freaks in school when I heard them inviting girls over to their houses and having sex with each other's victims. That's why I didn't give

Bryant the time of day. He would have sex with those girls and wouldn't call them afterward.

"Wait a minute, babe, you always brushing me off," he said.

Bryant got on his knees and asked me in front of everybody if he could take me out. He begged me. I finally gave in. I knew I wasn't giving up shit. I said yes, hoping he would get off his knees, embarrassing me. Saniyah and Mike walked down the hallway. He walked her to her locker and they both exchanged numbers.

I knew it was just a matter of time until they were going to be in the bed together. They both act just alike. Saniyah was classy like me, but had a strong sex drive and Mike he was just plain nasty. I was the closet type. I had sex before but I didn't enjoy it because it was painful. I broke my virginity at the age of 15.That didn't count to me, though, because the boy's cock was so small that I didn't bleed at all.

Bryant finally got off his knees and asked me to walk with him toward his locker. We then exchanged two way numbers. I told him that I worked in the evening and that he could not call my phone so late. He understood.

Bryant was so different to me; he was so handsome. For real, I just wanted to fuck him in the school building, but I knew if I got caught, my Dad would have killed me. I also knew that Mrs. Marilyn didn't play.

"I have to go Bryant. I will be late for English class. Come-on, Saniyah."

We walked to our English classes, taking the back stairway which was the quickest.

An hour later, lunch period was packed and everybody was so damned loud. I knew for some reason, Mike and Bryant was going to sit next to me and Saniyah. They sat next to us as soon as they walked in the cafeteria. Mike put his arms around Saniyah and Bryant tried to do the same with me.

I didn't budge. I let him because I wanted to see how long he would like me before I would have sex with him.

"So, Miss Jocelyn, how old are you," Bryant said to me.

"I am 17 years old, Bryant, how old are you?" I said to him.

"I am 18 years old, with no kids. This is your last year here, too, huh? Me and my family just moved in the area. I can't wait until graduation day, then off to college to play football." said Bryant.

"Oh, you like football," I replied back to him.

"Yes, baby, I practice every Saturday. If you not too busy, come watch me practice at the Recreation Center in Mid Towne. You know where that's at, right," said Bryant.

"Of course. I didn't just move around here, I am aware of the area," I said to him, giving him a mean expression on my face.

"Good, so when are we going to the movies?" said Bryant.

"This Friday I won't be working. I am off," I said to him.

"Cool, can I come and pick you up?" said Bryant.

"No, that wouldn't be a good idea. I will meet you somewhere. I am not comfortable letting anybody know where I live, out of respect," I said to him.

"Cool, let me go. I have gym, and then I am leaving. So, baby, call me later so we can talk- if you not to busy. I will be up waiting for that phone call," Bryant said, as he got out of the chair and walked away, smiling, showing those dimples and pretty ass teeth any girl could die for.

I must admit, I was kind of gullible because every time you turned around, I was thinking about him when Saniyah and I left the cafeteria.

I sent him a text. That was the text he would never forget and would often bring up in our arguments. Anyway, I walked into my ROTC class, which I hated. We had a test, so I turned my phone off to focus because I knew I needed this credit in order to graduate.

"Man, what's up with you and Miss Bourgeois Bitch?" said Mike.

"Who? Jocelyn?" said Bryant.

"Yes, nigga, you know who I am talking about. Man, you going to fuck or what? I can't wait to fuck her friend, Saniyah. She is a real freak if she is rolling like that, I guarantee Miss Bourgeois bitch rolls like that, too?" said Mike.

"Naw, not her. I can tell I am going to take it real slow. I want that to be wifey one day. She is beautiful and phat to death. She got pretty, natural, reddish-brown hair; all of her teeth is white, she short and thick and pretty. Yeah, that's wifey, bro. I am not fucking that one up. I want to get her ass pregnant," said Bryant.

"Man, you crazy. I am going to have my fun while I am young. Fuck these bitches. MOB, you know what that mean, money over bitches, my nigga," said Mike, giving Bryant dap.

"Nigga, you funny as shit. Somebody going to get your ass one day, you watch. I am out, man, I have to check on something for my mom. Let me sign out. I will call you tonight, my nigga," said Bryant.

"Bet, see you later, my nigga," said Mike.

Bryant signed out in the main office, went upstairs to his locker, grabbed his books, and left out of the school building, walking toward his 1996 Yukon dark blue truck. He pressed his alarm button, started his truck, and noticed a text message from Jocelyn which read.

Look, I don't play games at all. I am on the right track in my life right now, so if you think you are having sex with me on Friday, please, think twice. I am a hard-working girl; I am not one of these hoes chasing after you so think about it, if you want me, get it together. I need a settle down man. Are you that man? Let me know. Holler at your girl, playboy.

Bryant looked at his phone and smiled. *Wow, this girl is something else.* He drove off, heading toward his house where he lived with his mom and sister. Bryant's father had passed away two years ago and his mom has been depressed ever since. She needed that male role model around her and didn't want Bryant to leave her to go to college, but she knew that was her son's passion.

"Mom, are you home?" Bryant yelled, but there wasn't an answer. He walked toward the kitchen and read a note.

Baby, I am at the grocery store- couldn't wait for you. I didn't know if you were coming straight home from school. I am at the Giant at the Boulevard. Love, Mom

Bryant put the note down; left his books on the dining room table, and left out to meet his mom at the Giant grocery store ten minutes away from their house. He drove in the parking lot of the grocery store, spotted Sandra's car, and parked his truck behind her car. He walked out, heading toward the door.

Some woman stopped and said, "I know you-aren't you that basketball player, LeBron James?" She smiled.

"No, but thanks for the compliment. You must be Meagan Goode because you sure look just like her," he smiled.

"My name is Cindy." She shook his hand and smiled.

"I'm Bryant. I am in a rush right now; is there a number I can call you on some time," he said to her.

"I thought you would never ask." She handed him one of her business cards. Bryant looked at the card and noticed she worked at a massage spa on 59th Place. "Come see me some time," she said to him, as she switched away, walking toward her car.

Bryant could not resist temptation. He wanted to call her once he got home. He was very mature-looking for his age and would attract a lot of good-looking, older women.

"Mom, there you go." He saw Sandra in the line, getting ready to pay for the groceries.

"I got this," he pulled out his American Express credit card. The total came up to $147.96.

"You are so lucky to have a man to pay for your groceries," the clerk said to Sandra.

"Oh, no, baby, this is my son. Thanks, babe," Sandra said, smiling at Bryant.

"Anytime, Mom, I got you. Where is Mona?" he asked.

"You know your sister; she is probably with that no good ass boyfriend of hers. You know she is older now, I can't tell her what to do."

"She is 21 years old, so all I do is pray and leave it up to God," said Sandra.

They were walking toward the car. Bryant helped his mom with the grocery bags, putting all of them in her trunk, and then walked her toward the driver side of her car. He opened the door and closed it once she got in the car. He walked toward his truck and unlocked the doors with his keys. He got in, started the truck, and drove off after Sandra drove off.

When they drove up at the house, Mona was on the steps, crying with her hands on her face. Sandra parked the car in the drive way and got out.

"Mona," she yelled. "What happened now?"

Mona was still covering her face, crying. Bryant got out of the car quickly and walked toward Mona. He yelled, "Where the fuck is he at?"

Sandra yelled, "Bryant, calm down. I am sure Mona has another excuse she's going to tell us."

Mona looked up. Her eye was blacked and her lip was busted. Bryant yelled, "Did Ronny do this?"

"No, he didn't. Me and his baby mother got into a fight and I didn't want him to break it up, but he act like he was more on her side than mine."

"I don't know why I deal with him, Mom, but I love him," Mona said.

"I don't know why, either, Mona," Sandra said.

Sandra opened her trunk, grabbed some bags, and walked toward the door to put them on the kitchen counter table.

Bryant set beside Mona and said, "Sis, you older than me, how long are you going to put up with this?"

"I know, Bryant, not long. We women get fed up. I will wake up one day, I promise that to mom and you just wait and see."

Bryant gave her a hug, grabbed her hand, and walked her upstairs toward her room. "Sis, I love you," he said to her and Mona closed her door.

Bryant walked toward Sandra's trunk, opened it, and grabbed the rest of the bags. He put them on the kitchen counter top with the rest.

"I got this, baby; I will put the food up. Anything special you want me to cook you for dinner?" Sandra asked.

"Yes, a nice T-bone steak with mash potatoes and string beans," he replied.

"I sure will, baby," said Sandra.

Bryant looked at the clock. He was timing me to get off of work. I told him that I didn't want any late phone calls, so he was waiting for a right time. He walked upstairs and cut the shower on in Sandra's bedroom because Mona was in the other bathroom.

He took his clothes off; watching himself in the mirror and looking at his six pack, smiling. Bryant knew he was a sex symbol and girls would die to be with him. He had a sexy swagger to be his age. Bryant got in his misty, steaming hot shower, and his cell phone vibrated. He couldn't hear it because he was in the shower.

I said to myself, *oh well he probably over a girl house somewhere; I give up*. I drove up in front of CVS, got out, and turned my phone off. Keith was waiting for me, smiling.

"You are always on time," he said to me. I was hoping he said, "Let's go and fuck right now." I would have said, "Sure," and smiled at him.

I walked past him to hurry and up and clock in. Keith wanted me to go on the register because he knew I was able to work independently and always got my work done quickly.

We Became One
Chapter 3

I worked at CVS for two years, even after I graduated. But, of course, I quit. I saved up about $8,610. I wanted my own place, so I went to beauty school, taking cosmetology for a year, and after that my next step was that I moved out of my parent's house.

I was on my way to college before I went to trade school until my Dad got sick and was diagnosed with lung cancer. I stayed with my mom for a couple of weeks to help with him.

Bryant and I were in a deep relationship. He went off to a trade school for culinary and, after that, he graduated, receiving his certificate. He was now a professional chef. Who would have ever thought Bryant would be a cook? But, he was very good at it.

Bryant lived by himself in a two-bedroom condo loft in Upper Marlboro, Maryland with his dog, Rocky. I moved closer to him in the Clinton, Maryland area. I rented a two-bedroom townhouse. I knew, one day, that he and I would live together. I thought it was better this way until we got married and had our family, but if Bryant had told me to pack up and come live with him, I would have moved out of my townhome quickly.

I called his phone and he answered with his deep voice.

"Hey, baby, what's up? What are you doing, sexy?" I asked him.

"Out with a couple of my friends, that's about it," said Bryant.

"I was on my way to you, but wanted to see if it was okay if I come over," I asked him.

"Come on, baby, why you are asking a stupid question like that? You know you always welcome," said Bryant. "I will be home. Use your key; I love you," he said, before we hung the phone up.

Rushing, I grabbed a pair of my sexy lingerie, comfortable slippers, and robe. I knew I didn't need anything else. I had not seen him in a week and I couldn't wait. I turned off every light off in the house except for the lights in the living room and my bedroom light. I always kept those lights on.

I fed my cat named Diamond, grabbed my iPod and iPod stand, and left the house. I knew I had forgotten something, but couldn't put my finger on it. *Ooh, I know my sex toys*. I knew what Bryant liked. I grabbed my vibrator for myself and anal ease for him.

I started my 745 BMW that my mom bought me for my 21st birthday two months ago. My navigation system took me where I needed to go and Bryant lived thirty minutes from me. I wanted to be there before he came home so I could make him a quick meal. He didn't eat red meat anymore so I grilled pepper chicken for him, steamed vegetables, and a baked potato.

I knew he had a freezer full of food, so I finally drove up in front of his beautiful complex. It was a gated community, so I keyed in my code to get inside of the gates. I loved that safety for Bryant because of his work schedule.

Once I got to the building of his condo, 512, I drove toward his driveway, got out, and pressed the code to open his garage. I got back in my car and drove the car inside his garage, turned the ignition off and lights, walked inside the opened building, got on the elevator to the 5th floor, and walked to door 512.I opened the door using my key.

Bryant kept everything so neat and smelling so fresh that it smelled like Febreze. I hurried up the stairs into his master bedroom. Bryant had a room any girl would die for. His king-sized, sleigh bed was so comfortable and neatly tucked in. I lit his candles on his wall in the candle set I bought him last month, plugged my iPod up, and put it on his dresser to begin playing love making songs by Tevin Campbell, Prince, R Kelly, and Keith Sweat. That drove him crazy.

The first time we made love was in his old truck. I gave in. I ended up giving him some after the third date. I couldn't resist temptation and he fucked my brains out that night, which made me whipped.

His home phone ranged and I crept toward the kitchen. It went to his voicemail and a lady named Cindy left a message, sounding very seductive.

"Bryant, this is Cindy, we have to meet tomorrow. I have something you may be interested in. Call me so we can meet somewhere. Talk to you soon, bye bye.

Beep

I wasn't mad. I knew Bryant wouldn't cheat on me and it sounded like it was important, pertaining to his business, so I left it alone. I never brought that call to his attention because I knew he would deny it anyway.

I turned on the shower water after opening the clear, French, glass shower doors. I noticed three wash cloths on the top of his shower. I thought maybe he didn't realize he already had a wash cloth.

I rushed through my shower so I could be out before Bryant came home. Once I got out. I wiped the steam from the mirror and noticed two tooth brushes. Now I was really puzzled, but I still didn't want to question him because I didn't want to start an argument.

I looked at my hair which was nice and pretty. I dyed my hair this beautiful raspberry color and it looked good on my caramel skin.

I walked inside Bryant's room and opened his armoire. I noticed a porn DVD on the top of his DVD player. It's normal for a man to watch porn so I grabbed the cocoa butter and lotioned my skin down. My feet were nicely pedicured. My nails were freshly done. I wrapped my hair with another towel to towel dry it and give it that wet-set look. My hair used to come down my back until I cut it into a bobbed style. My hair was naturally soft. I got that from my mom.

I put on my lingerie, see-through dress with my black thong, and wore my slippers to walk around the house. I let the towel go and grabbed my Louis Vuitton purse to put my MAC makeup and my lip glass on to shine my full, plumped lips. I sprayed some of my Britney Spears perfume and walked toward the kitchen, waiting for the chicken to defrost.

I opened a bag of vegetables, turned the oven on 350, and grabbed two potatoes. I put holes in them so they could cook fast, grabbed a flat pan, and put the potatoes in the oven.

I seasoned the vegetables and turned the stove on. I straightened up the living room area, putting his gym bag in his walk-in closet in the hallway. Dinner would be ready in 30 minutes. I lit the candles on the table and grabbed two plates from the dishwasher, along with two spoons, two knives, and two forks. I laid them neatly on the table with some napkins and then went to go check on the vegetables. The aroma had the house smelling good.

I heard keys at the door. *My baby is home*, I said to myself as I walked toward the living room. There he was like a chocolate candy bar, so sexy and tall. My pussy was throbbing as soon as I saw him. He had that effect on me!

"Hey, baby." He grabbed me, picked me up, and gave me a long kiss. "I missed you." Bryant said. He took my mind off what I was going to ask him.

"I am dirty, baby; I was at the park with the homies.I need to get in the shower," he said.

"I know, baby, dinner is almost ready," I said to him.

I walked toward the kitchen, my ass jiggling everywhere.

Bryant looked at me, undressing me with his eyes, and then he walked toward his bedroom. I poured us a glass of wine-White Zinfandel. The potatoes and vegetables were ready. The chicken was almost ready, but it needed another 10 minutes to cook.

Bryant opened the glass doors, turned the shower water on, and got in the shower. I tip-toed in his bedroom while waiting for the chicken to finish cooking. I reached inside his pants pocket and grabbed his Black Berry cell phone. He had 22 unread text messages. I thought to myself, *hmmm!*

I knew if I would have read it, he would have found out that I was looking in his phone would have said something to me. He had three missed calls five minutes ago. Bryant was known for being a player back in high school, but I never caught him doing anything. After looking at his phone for fifteen minutes, I put it back in his pocket because I heard the water turn off in the shower.

I tip-toed out of the room and walked downstairs toward the kitchen. The chicken was finally done. I put both glasses of wine on the dining room table and fixed both of our plates. Bryant walked downstairs, wearing only a towel wrapped around his waist, showing his six-pack on his brown, beautiful, shiny skin.

He sat and said, "Baby, you know I have to travel to Atlanta next month for a meeting. I might get this contract with one of the most famous restaurants down in ATL called Saskatoon, located on 360 Pharr Rd, northeast of Atlanta, GA."

"Babe, they are looking for a chef?"

"I have to prepare three good meals so they can make their decision," he said.

"That's good. What about me, Bryant? You know I love you, how I can trust you?" I asked him.

He cut a piece of his chicken and potatoes and said, "Baby, this is good and the vegetables are delicious."

"Don't fucking skip the subject," I yelled.

"I am not, babe, go look inside of my pants pocket," he said.

I got up from the table so quick and walked fast toward the bedroom. I reached down in his back pants pocket and pulled out a box. *I know he didn't*, I said to myself. I brought the box back to him and opened it.

My eyes got so big. It was the double diamond bracelet I wanted from Jared and printed in the inside, it said, Diamond Princess. That was Bryant's nickname for me when we were making love.

I never heard him call me Diamond Princess in public. I cried and grabbed his face to suck on his lips. Bryant got up and carried me to his bedroom. I could not wait until he laid me on the bed. He kissed my neck, kissed my perky breasts, then down to my inner thighs, giving me foreplay.

Bryant sucked on my clitoris so hard and slow while opening my legs up wide so he could suck all of my juices for about 10 minutes. I enjoyed all of the pleasure.

I lifted my body up because his turn was next. He deserved to have his cock sucked after that gift I received. I couldn't wait to have him inside my mouth. I slowly pulled his big, thick cock out from the towel and put my mouth on it fast. I slowly sucked his hard cock nonstop. Bryant moaned so loud I could taste his pre-cum inside my mouth.

I went up and down, locking my jaws on his big, black cock. After five minutes, Bryant wanted to enter me from behind, grinding my wet, sugar walls and palming my round ass in his hands.

I moaned out loud. He went in deeper and deeper, nonstop. I wanted to take control at this point. I wanted to ride his cock up and down. I got on top of him, grabbed my satin scarf from out of his night stand, and drew and tied his hands together while riding him. Bryant turned the iPod on his favorite song, R Kelly's "*It Seems Like You Ready*". Bryant loved when I danced to that song. He always fantasized me on the pole because he knew I had special moves.

I grinded and grinded on him until he couldn't resist any more. Bryant climaxed in my love so strongly my stomach cramped for hours that night. I conceived my kids.

The Breaking News
Chapter 4

"Damn, these babies are killing my back," I said to my mother.

"When I was pregnant with you, I couldn't wait until you came out. You were making me sick for the whole DAMNED nine months," Marilyn said.

"Baby, I have something to tell you and I don't want you to get upset, baby girl, but your dad is not going to live long. His cancer has spread throughout his body. He is at his last stage. There is nothing the doctors can do at this point. He went through chemo and is just waiting for God to take him home. He already had been to the hospital twice this week. He stated to the family that he didn't want to be resuscitated, keeping him alive," Marilyn said.

"Mom, don't say that. I am going to talk to him," I said, very angry at my mom.

I remember walking toward the bedroom and watching my dad sleep. You could tell he was sick because of the amount of weight he had lost. His face was sunken in.

"Dad," I called his name and he opened his eyes.

"Baby, I remember when you first called me dad. That was your first word when you were one year old.

I'll never forget your mom was upset that mom wasn't your first word," Steven said to her, smiling and coughing at the same time.

"I am so sorry, Daddy, that I have not seen you in two months. I usually come see you and Mom every month, but these babies been wearing me down."

"I am having twins, Dad, and Bryant is so excited," I said to him, as tears rolled down my face.

My dad said, "Baby girl, you know I love you. I am sick. You make sure you send my grandkids off to colleges and make sure they are taken care of for the rest of their lives. You know Daddy took care of you right with my policy," Steven said.

"Dad, I'd rather have you than money. Nobody can ever replace you, "I said to him, crying. I lay beside him, held him tightly, and dozed off to sleep.

My mom walked in, tucked me and him under the cover, and cried while watching us sleep. She loved her some Steven and he loved her.

My dad died the next day. Those were my last words to him. He had fallen in love with Bryant the first time he met him. He gave him a father-in-law speech and told him if he ever hurt me, he would kill him, even if he was dead. He would haunt him in his sleep and scare the hell out of him. Bryant laughed and laughed in tears.

My dad was buried in Arlington Cemetery in Arlington, Virginia. All of my family came out and Bryant was by me and my mom's side. My mother cried so much that she didn't have any more tears left in her. After my dad was buried, we had a memorial at my mom's house. Bryant and I stayed for a while, but we had to go to the hotel to catch our flight the next day.

Bryant and I moved closer to his job, which was in Atlanta, and that's when pretty much the cheating began. The twins were born two months after my dad passed away. I named them Aniyah and Eniyah Nicole Carter after my best friend Saniyah Nicole. They were six pounds and 14 ounces.

My mother flew down from Virginia and stayed with us for about two months, helping me put with the twins because Bryant's work schedule was pretty tied up. He was hardly ever home.

I received a called from the house phone. "Hello," I answered. Nobody said anything; they hung-up. It rang again. I answered, "Hello," and still no one answered. When I tried to press star 69, the phone number was blocked.

My mother saw the expression on my face. This had never happened before. We had only lived in Atlanta for a couple of months and nobody really knew our number. Maybe it was the wrong number or someone's phone may have lost signal.

I called Bryant's phone and it went straight to voicemail.

"Hey, baby, I was just checking on you. I miss you. Me and the babies are getting ready for bed. I hope to see you tonight, love."

I hung up the phone. Marilyn walked toward the twin's bedroom to check on them and they were quietly sleeping. She closed the door and walked inside my bedroom to tell me goodnight.

"I love you," my mom said to me.

"I love you, too, Mom. Thanks for being here with me," I said to her.

I wanted to cry but I remained strong. Bryant was hardly ever there, but he was holding the bills down. My mom split the policy up, 500,000 thousand apiece and we almost ran through the money fast. The house was 200,000 thousand, which was cheap for a five-bedroom, brick, two-car garage, four full bathrooms, three-level house with a big deck on the kitchen and a big, fenced backyard.

I bought Bryant a new Mercedes Benz with smoked out rims and sun roof. That car was only 35,000 dollars. I paid straight out, plus I had his 2000 Denali truck he bought as soon as we moved to Atlanta. I still had my 745 BMW. It was often parked because I never really went anywhere but to the store and back home.

I needed a full makeover. I knew I had to take a visit to Bryant's office sooner or later, like how I used to do when he was the chef at the restaurant. Bryant was now the Vice Owner of Sasketoon restaurant under Mr. Ricky Nelson, the owner. I grabbed my laptop and looked up a personal trainer. I felt fat. While my mother was there, I was going to work out three times a week to get my figure back.

Love Affairs
Chapter 5

The house phone rang again and this time it was Sandra. "Hello, Miss Lady, how are you and my grandbabies?"

"We are fine, Sandra, thanks for asking. My mom is here helping me out," I said to her.

"I know, Bryant, told you I am coming up there next month to help out with my grandbabies."

"You know I am the only one here. Mona moved to Chicago with her husband, so I am here all by myself."

"I left a message on Bryant's phone."

"I am sure he will respond."

"I know he is busy at work, so I didn't want to bother him. You take care of yourself. I love you and kiss my babies for me," said Sandra.

"I will, Sandra." Then, I hung the phone up.

I Google personal trainer on the internet in this area and I found one. He was very reasonable which was good for me, but I really didn't care at this point. I felt fat and unattractive. My ass was so big and my breasts were double Ds. I couldn't wait to start. I emailed him so fast and he responded quickly. He asked when I could start and I told him tomorrow morning.

I responded bright and early. He responded at 7:30 in the morning and left his address. I closed my laptop and went downstairs to prepare the twins' milk so my mother wouldn't need anything else for them. It was now 3:00 a.m. in the morning.

I heard some keys at the front door and it was my baby. He looked tired. "Hey, baby," I said to him.

"Hey, babe, why are you still up? It's late," said Bryant.

"I was up waiting for you, babe," I said to him.

When Bryant walked past, I smelled the scent of Bath and Body Works Vanilla Brown Sugar on his clothes. I attempted to give him a hug and he moved my arms quickly and went straight to the bathroom.

"Baby, I am tired. I worked overtime tonight. Let me take a quick shower and lay down, please, babe," he said to me.

Usually, Bryant would kiss me as soon as he walked in the door, but ever since we moved to Atlanta and I had the babies, everything went downhill. Our love didn't feel the same. I left it alone because whatever is done in the dark will soon come to light, and when it does, Bryant is going to be in trouble.

I walked upstairs after preparing the babies' milk, got in the bed, tucked myself under the cover, and went to sleep. I had four hours to work out and it had been a long time. I wanted so badly to go snooping in Bryant's cell phone, but I didn't. I also didn't want my mother to notice anything and cause an argument. My mother always said when you go snooping, looking for something; you may just get a surprise.

I wasn't ready for that. The next morning, I got up to get dressed to go work out when Bryant turned around and asked, "Where are you going? I am off today. I wanted to spend some time with you, babe."

"I have a meeting," I said to him.

"With whom?" he asks.

"With a client who wants their hair done," I said to him.

"This time of morning, Jocelyn? What the fuck you play me for?" he yelled out. I grabbed my tank top and my spandex Adidas sweat suit, my New Balance and grabbed my keys, gave him a kiss on his head, and walked down the stairs. I put the code in the alarm system and walked out the front door to warm up my car in the garage.

While the car was warming up, I quickly ran back inside, turned the alarm off, and walked into the kitchen to make me some coffee. The twins were up and started crying. Bryant walked downstairs and heated them up their bottles. While I was making my coffee, he started talking and being disrespectful.

I ignored him. He said, "I guess you off to meet your boyfriend, huh, sneaky ass bitch," he mumbled.

I gave him an innocent look and said, "Baby, I would never cheat on you. I love you too much."

I grabbed my cup of coffee and left out of the garage door.

"Good morning," Marilyn said to Bryant.

"Good morning, Mom," he said to her as he kissed her cheek.

"What are you all arguing about early this morning?" she said to Bryant

"Nothing, Mom, its minor. Don't mind us; I am just stressing out at the job. I think I am going to take some time off to spend time with my family. I put my vacation time in already for next month because my mom is flying down to come help out with the twins," said Bryant.

"I know having babies is very stressful. They are young right now but as soon as they get older, you will miss them being young again," said Marilyn.

She grabbed the bottles from Bryant's hand and walked up the stairs. Bryant wanted to make a special breakfast for Jocelyn and Marilyn, so he grabbed some eggs to make an omelet and then grabbed the turkey bacon and butter milk biscuits. His cell phone rang.

"Good morning, babe, did you enjoy last night?" said Cindy.

He whispered, "I sure did, sir. When can we meet again?" said Bryant. Trying to pretend that she was a man.

"I hope tonight, daddy," said Cindy.

"Nope, that's going to be a problem. I can't see you tonight. Maybe Friday night."

"I can't be late two nights in a row. You know Jocelyn not having that," Bryant said to her.

"That's not your wife yet, you can do whatever you want to do, baby," said Cindy.

"I have to go now. I'll text you later and don't call my phone back today," he whispered.

"Okay, baby, I won't," Cindy replied back to him.

He hung the phone up and began to prepare breakfast.

"Here comes the Bride" Mrs. Carter Chapter 6

Three years later, me and Bryant got married. He proposed to me in front of my family and friends. It was at Mike's 25th birthday party. I was so excited. He took out a small red box that had a 14-carat diamond cluster ring that matched the diamond bracelet he bought me three years ago.

Bryant made a toast with his wine glass and raised his expensive bottle of Dom Perignon. He got on one knee, proposed and gave this long speech.

"Baby, I know I have not been the perfect man these past years, but I swear to you I can change. Nothing else in this world can make me happy but you. Please be my wife 'til death do us part. I love you, baby. Please be my wife and marry me," Bryant says to me.

That speech sticks with me to this day. It still brings tears to my eyes because that's all a woman can ever dream about, a big, beautiful wedding and a good husband.

I couldn't say no although I was mad at him the night before. But, that all went out the door again. We had a big wedding in Jamaica, Montego Bay with only 100 guests invited. Mike and Bryant paid for everybody to participate.

I was so fit and in shape for my wedding day. My ass was tight and my wedding dress was satin, pearl-white and fit all of my natural curves, thanks to my personal trainer. He made sure I was right for my day.

The bridesmaid's dress was pretty lavender. Saniyah was my bridesmaid and, of course, Mike was Bryant's best man. My mom was so proud of her baby girl that she cried and cried; it was a joyful experience. We spent our reception on a Carnival Cruise to Aruba for six days and seven nights. I never thought Bryant could be so romantic. That whole week I fell in love with him all over again. Nothing could ever break us apart, nothing. I was now Mrs. Jocelyn Carter.

Two months later, in 2005, the kids went to their grandmother's house in Virginia for the summer. I needed that break so Bryant and I could spend some time to ourselves. Sandra was so excited because she couldn't wait until she saw her grandkids. The girls where older now, they just had their 4th birthday party together at Chuck E. Cheese's two weeks ago and she was so anxiously waiting to get them.

Mona flew down from Chicago to spend time with her nieces since she had not seen them in four years. She loved their pretty, long, red-brownish hair and their pretty smile, with those deep dimples like their father. Mona had those dimples, also. The twins could be her kids. Because they looked so much like their dad, they also had their aunt in them.

I went back to work, but only worked four days out of the week and by appointment. My four days were pretty booked with my regular clients. My phone was ringing daily and I was getting a high volume of emails.

I purchased a salon and was now the owner. The shop was called Hair of Elegance and it was the best hair salon in Atlanta Georgia downtown. The salon had loyal workers and often did hair shows every six months which brought a lot of clientele.

One day, I decided to get jazzy and fly on my day off. I dyed my hair again, only this time, the color was honey blond. I added a few pieces in my hair so it could look fuller and lengthy.

I put my MAC makeup and red lipstick on. I decided to take a visit to Bryant's office downtown in Atlanta in one of the professional building. I wore my tight, fitted black and grey pencil skirt and suit jacket with my snakeskin, Nine West pumps along with my Dolce & Gabbana handbag. I drove up to Bryant's job and parked my car in one of Bryant's personal parking spaces. I walked to the elevator and took it to the 5th floor.

I saw the receptionist at the desk on the phone. She didn't recognize me. She may have thought I worked there because of how I was professionally dressed. I walked in front of his office door and opened it. A woman was sitting there in front of his desk with her legs crossed and looked very petite and young. Bryant was sitting in front of her with his hands on her leg. I noticed this woman had on the same bracelet that Bryant brought me three years ago that matched my wedding ring.

"Hello, Bryant," I said. They both looked at me

"Hey, baby, what are you doing here?" Bryant said, looking suspicious.

"I came to take you to lunch, but I see you already have a date with this bitch right now," I yelled.

"Hi, I am Cindy." She sounded so seductive. "I am sorry you are upset. We were in a meeting-you are Jocelyn, right?" Cindy said.

"Yes, Mrs. Jocelyn Carter, his wife," I said to her, showing my cluster wedding ring.

"I heard a lot about you, come in and have a seat. I was just leaving," said Cindy.

"Yes, I think you should leave," I said to her, giving her straight eye contact.

I couldn't wait to hear another excuse from Bryant so, once Cindy left, I closed the door.

"Let me explain something to you. Don't you ever come in my office again and embarrass me," Bryant yelled.

"Oh, you called that embarrassing? When I can't get a good fuck at home or a fucking date?"

I pointed my finger to him in rage.

"I am trying to support us and our family you don't have the right to pop up here. Don't fucking do it again, bitch," Bryant threatened me.

"Or what, Bryant, what are you going to do? Do me a favor and stop coming home smelling like her scent, "I said to him in rage, walking away and opening his door. I slammed his glass door while he was standing with his hands on his hips. The glass shattered everywhere. I didn't care. I knew Bryant was having an affair, but I just couldn't put my finger on it.

Caught up
Chapter 7

"Meet me at the Cafe on 24thAvenue, I may have some information you might want to hear and see," Saniyah said to me.

"Girl, I give up. Is it something about Bryant because I am tired," I said to her.

"Just come down here; get your butt up," said Saniyah.

"All right, let me slip something on, I will be there," I said.

"Hurry up, you should want to see this for yourself," said Saniyah.

What did this girl want, I said to myself. I slipped on a pair of my Parasuco Jeans, my DKNY fitted black shirt, my flat, ballerina shoes, and grabbed my Fendi purse with my Prada sunglasses.

I turned the ignition on my car up and drove out of the car garage. I had not talked to Bryant for a week after the argument. We decided to give each other space for a while and maybe work things out before the twins came home next month.

I parked my car in the parking lot across the street from the café and walked across the street. I saw Saniyah's car parked in front of the café. I walked to her table and sat across from her.

"Okay, what's wrong, Saniyah? You scared me half to death what," I asked her.

"Walk like you are going to the bathroom. Bryant is here with that woman and they come here every Thursday in the morning time and sit and hold hands. I even saw them kiss. They just did it five minutes ago," said Saniyah.

"Okay, I am getting ready to catch his ass."

I walked toward the bathroom and took my glasses off.

"Hello, Bryant, and Cindy, right?" I said to them both.

I caught them tongue kissing like they were making a porn movie. I didn't want to hear Bryant's excuse. I was tired. I took my wedding ring off and threw it at him. It landed right in front of him and that was the end for me. I left out, crying.

"Thanks, Saniyah," I said to her, while leaving out of the café.

Bryant chased after me.

"Babe, wait, it's not what you think." Bryant ran toward me across the street, not paying attention. I stopped upon hearing the sound of his voice. I turned my head and a car hit me, going 45mph. I closed my eyes. I thought I was already dead.

Bryant paused. He stood in the middle of the street to stop traffic. The elderly woman that was driving the car got out and said, "Are you okay, lady?"

She and Bryant ran to my side and Bryant called the ambulance on my phone.

"911, what's your emergency?" the dispatcher said.

"My wife was hit by a car, please help me, she is bleeding to death."

"Sir, what's your location?" the dispatcher asked.

"I am at 24thAvenue, Atlanta, Georgia, hurry," Bryant said, sounding nervous

"The ambulance is en route to you, sir, they will be there in ten minutes," said the dispatcher.

Bryant hung the phone up and lifted my head which was covered with blood. My leg was bent. My arm was twisted. I couldn't feel anything and I blanked out. I woke up in the hospital bed, surrounded by nurses, and Bryant was there by me.

"Babe, I am sorry for cheating on you with Cindy," he said.

"Baby, I love you. I would never hurt you again. If you want to move, we can we can sell the house-do whatever you want to do, baby, I am sorry," Bryant said.

I looked at him and shook my head. I couldn't talk because I had a tube down my throat. Tears ran down my face. I believed him this time, but why did it take this to happen to me for Bryant to change.

Bryant said, "I called both of our mothers. Marilyn is catching a flight here. I have to pick her up at the airport tomorrow. Baby, I don't ever want to lose you." He reached down in his pocket, grabbed my wedding ring, put it on my finger, and kissed me on my forehead. I was relieved.

I had been going to therapy for six months now. Bryant was the perfect man again. He stayed home with me for two months after the accident and then he had to go back to work. I was doing hair at home. I still owned my shop. Bryant bought two restaurants from what was left from my dad's insurance money and we were living well. Our business was booming.

I let Saniyah be in charge of the shop while I was recovering. My cell phone vibrated and it was a nice text from Bryant saying his daily quote: *God has sent me an angel. I love you, baby*. I responded back texting, saying that I love him, too. I was so glad I was walking again. I suffered mild injuries, but nothing major. I knew God was definitely looking after me that day. My right leg was fractured and my arm was fractured, too, but there wasn't any internal bleeding. I knew me and Bryant needed a vacation, just me and him. We decided to go to Las Vegas for a week before the girls came home.

On the plane ride there, I laid my head on his shoulder. His phone vibrated when he received a text message from a woman named Michelle Humphries. Bryant was asleep because we had already have been on the plane for two hours. I knew he couldn't wait to get to our hotel room which was the MGM. I trusted my husband this time, so I didn't read the text because he promised that he wouldn't cheat again. I wouldn't know what I would of do if I caught him having sex with another woman. Although he confessed to me that he and Cindy were seeing each other, he said that it was so long ago.

I knew he and Cindy were fucking because one, his scent, two, them in the office, and three, at the café. What more could I see? Bryant told me one time to bark like a dog. I barked and got on my knees during sex. I was his love slave bitch that night. We were into role-playing and shit and I liked that freaky side of him that drove me crazy. I pushed his cell phone deeper in his pocket. He must have felt it because he woke right up and said, "baby, is everything okay?"

I looked at him and said, "everything is everything, babe."

He looked at me and smiled and then we both rested our eyes and dozed off to sleep. The MGM was so elegant and beautiful. The cab let us off in front of the hotel. The bell boys grabbed our luggage, walked toward the front desk, and said, "Reservation for Mr. Bryant Carter," with his deep voice.

The concierge looked in the computer and said, "yes, you have the king bed, guestroom suite, correct?"

"Yes," Bryant replied back.

He gave us our hotel swipe card keys and then we proceeded to walk toward the elevator. The bell boy got on a separate elevator because of the amount of luggage we had. When we got off the elevator, we walked to suite number 512.What a coincidence, the same number of Bryant's old condo in Upper Marlboro.

Bryant wanted to surprise me so he asked me to open the door. I attempted to open the suite door. It was beautiful. The suite had a 51-inch LCD flat screen TV mounted on the wall in the living room area and the smell of fresh leather smelled so fresh to me. The kitchen counter was granite with cement tile on the floor, like our house's kitchen floor. We walked toward the fireplace that was lit. It was an electric fire place and that was so beautiful. When I walked toward the bedroom, mirrors were everywhere-on the ceiling, on the walls, and the bathroom was inside of the bedroom. The bathroom was so big that it came with a heart-shaped, big Jacuzzi tub. I turned the water on in the Jacuzzi while Bryant went to pour us a glass of wine.

I walked in the bedroom and unpacked. I laid my red lingerie set out on the bed that I had just bought from Victoria's Secret, pulled out my Frederick's of Hollywood silver sandals, and grabbed my diamond choker and diamond bracelet. I never questioned Bryant about the bracelet that Cindy wore. I knew he was going to deny that he bought it, so I stopped wearing mine after that incident. Too many memories and bad thoughts.

I suddenly had a flashback. I took a deep breath and grabbed my body spray, brown sugar and fig, and walked back in the bathroom. I stopped the water from running and sprayed my body spray in the air and in the Jacuzzi area. Bryant walked in and handed me my glass of wine. I put the glass down and got undressed. My nipples were so hard. Bryant loved my naked, caramel body and he had no reason to go anywhere else. He held my hand and I dipped my feet in the water to make sure it wasn't too hot. It was just right. I got into the Jacuzzi, waiting for Bryant. He took his white T-shirt off, unzipped his pants, pulled his boxers down slowly, then his socks, and got in the Jacuzzi tub with me. He sipped his glass of wine and then we made a toast to new beginnings. After that toast, we started to make passionate love. I stroked his hard shaft up and down until his juices began to flow. I stood in front of him while he was laying back. I got on top of his rock-hard cock slowly, grabbing his ears and sucking his bottom lip at the same time. Moving my hips round and round in circles, I was riding him slowly, and he moaned while gripping my ass. We tongue kissed for minutes. The water was so warm and you could hear the sound of the water moving back and forth. Bryant sucked my nipples, putting a hickey on my breast. We made love for an hour in the bathroom and then took it to the bedroom. That was the best night ever. We enjoyed our time in Las Vegas. We gambled almost every day and lost all of our money. I couldn't wait until I got home. I missed the twins.

Detective Mack said to Jocelyn that he wanted to take a 20-minute break. The tape stopped and he put another tape in for the next session

"Jocelyn, I have to put the handcuffs back on you for safety purposes. Don't worry, I am coming right back, did you want me to bring you some coffee back with a straw? I have to leave these handcuffs on you if you want some coffee," said Detective Mack.

"That's fine, Detective Mack, I appreciate it," said Jocelyn.

Tears rolled down Jocelyn's face as Detective Mack walked out of the break room and down the hallway to the kitchen. This story was getting to him emotionally although he was used to these stories. He felt sorry for Jocelyn. He knew she didn't mean to kill her husband; she had just gotten tired of Bryant lying to her and cheating. She was enraged.

Ten minutes came and Detective Mack walked into the room with a cup of coffee. He added sugar and cream and put the cup down in front of Jocelyn with a straw. Jocelyn took a sip and said, "Just the way I like it. Thanks, I appreciate this."

Detective Mack sat in the chair across from her, took the first tape out of the cassette, put it in his suit jacket, and put another tape in the tape recorder.

"Are you ready to begin the next session, Jocelyn?" said Detective Mack.

"Yes, ready to get it over with," Jocelyn replied.

Detective Mack pressed record and play, and then Jocelyn began talking.

He Loves Me Not
Chapter 8

Aniyah and Eniyah walked in with Bryant's mom. They yelled and ran toward me. "Mommy, I missed you!"

I grabbed them and held them tightly. "Mommy has a surprise for you both."

"What is it, Mommy?" Eniyah said.

"Well, let's get dressed and have mommy and daughters day at the spa."

"Okay," the girls replied back. They ran upstairs in their room and grabbed their outfits from out of the closet. They wanted to wear their new Baby Phat sweat suits and white Nike tennis shoes Bryant bought them while they were gone.

I walked upstairs and Bryant walked behind me. "Babe, you smell good. What is that new scent called?" he said.

"What new scent? It's the same body spray I wore in Las Vegas, babe," I said to him, giving him a strange look.

"I will be here when you and the girls get back. I am going to prepare dinner for the family, so don't be too long," Bryant said.

I was dressed to kill that day. I also wore my Baby Phat light pink velour sweat suit and fresh, pink, yellow, and white Nike tennis shoes. My sweat suit had Baby Phat written on the back of my jacket.

"Come on, girls, let's go!" I yelled upstairs. My daughters where such little ladies. They got themselves dressed; helping each other put their clothes on. The girls ran downstairs and waved their hand bye to Bryant.

"No kiss?" Bryant said to them both. They both ran to him and gave him a big hug and kiss. I opened the door and gave Bryant a kiss on his cheek.

"Ladies, let's go, we have an appointment." We got in the car and I said to them, "Don't forget to put your seatbelt on, girls."

Aniyah and Eniyah buckled their seatbelts and I buckled mine, too, and then drove off. I wanted to take them to the spa downtown around the corner from my shop. I drove for about 30 minutes and drove up at the spa called *Atlanta's Finest.* It was packed, but we had an appointment, so we were seen as soon as we walked in the door. We walked downstairs to the spa room which only had two people there. Mrs. Pat walked Aniyah and Eniyah to the pedicure chair and I walked to the manicure chair, so she could start on my nails while Mrs. Brown did the girls' feet at the same time.

"Mommy, this feels great," Aniyah said. Eniyah was sitting back reading a magazine like she knew what she was reading.

Ring Ring

"Hello," Bryant answered.

"Well, hello, stranger," said Michelle. "You have been ducking my calls lately. Long time, no see."

"What's up, Michelle, how can I help you?" said Bryant.

"I have a proposal I want you to look at. Do you have time to come out to see me in an hour?" said Michelle.

"Yes, let me get dressed. Where do you want me to meet you?" said Bryant.

"Our normal spot, Hilton conference center. I have it available for three hours. Hurry up and get down," her she demanded.

"I'm on my way. I'll be there in 20 minutes," he said and hung the phone up.

He met Michelle at a business retreat for all chefs. She was the Marketing Specialist. Michelle always had the hot for him. She was tall, dark, lovely, and petite, with a plump ass. She wore a pinstriped grey and white suit with her breasts pushed up, boots, tie, bra, and grey satin BCBG pumps she got from Neiman Marcus.

She sat at the conference table waiting for Bryant to walk through the door. She had it all planned out to seduce him as soon as he walked in.

"I hope this is fast. I have to hurry up home to prepare dinner," he said to her.

"Have a seat," said Michelle. She poured him and her a glass of wine, White Zinfandel, and sat his glass in front of him. Michelle was a woman any man could die for. Her black, long hair was so chic and her skin was smooth and shiny. She was so pretty, just like the model Naomi Campbell, very tall and pretty.

Bryant sat beside her and said, “Where are the proposals?”

Michelle got up, walked toward the conference door and locked it, holding her glass of wine in her hand. She took a big gulp of her glass of wine and walked toward him, unbuttoning her jacket, showing her black bustier and perky breasts.

Bryant smiled and said, “Ooh, is that what you wanted me here for, huh?”

Michelle grabbed Bryant’s face, leaned over to him, put her tongue in his mouth, and started massaging his hard shaft through his pants.

“I got to go,” he said. He stood up. She grabbed his hands and put them on her breasts, making him massage her perky breasts.

“I want you, Bryant,” she whispered in his hears. She nibbled on his ear lobe and started kissing his neck, then down his chest, lifting his shirt up. She got on her knees and started sucking on his belly button and his six-pack abs. She then took his sweat pants down to his knees and grabbed his hard cock.

“Michelle, “He said. She opened her mouth wide and started sucking on the head of his cock, then instantly deep-throating his shaft up and down, slowly, then fast. Bryant could not resist temptation. He grabbed the back of her neck and made her suck him even harder. Juices came out of her mouth, landing on her chest. She spit on his cock, and then began sucking it while jerking his cock back and forth at the same time for about ten minutes. Michelle laid Bryant on the conference table, climbed on top of him, and inserted his hard cock inside her wet, tight pussy. She rode Bryant slowly, moaning out loud. It felt so good to her. Michelle finally got what she wanted from Bryant. He then took control and flipped her on her back, opening her legs wide and pounding her in and out, nonstop.

"Oooooooh,awwwwwww!"She moaned and moaned until he climaxed inside of her.

Michelle slid off of the table and sucked his juices from out of his cock. She sucked and sucked until there wasn't a drop left. Bryant looked at his watch and said, "Sorry, I have to go." He pulled his pants up and walked toward the front door to unlock it. Then, he went in the men's bathroom outside the conference room and washed the scent from his cock in the sink and dried it off with a paper towel.

"Come on, girls, we have to make it home like daddy said. You know he is preparing dinner for us," I said to the girls.

Eniyah and Aniyah got in the car and put their seat belts on.

"Come on, Mommy, I can't wait until Daddy sees my nails and my feet design," said Aniyah.

Driving for about 30 minutes, I finally drove up in front of the house and said to myself, *where is Bryant? He said he wasn't going anywhere*. So, I called his phone.

Ring Ring

"Babe, I am at the grocery store, I am sorry, we don't have any more milk. I am just down the street. I wanted to make the girls their favorite mashed potatoes. I left the boneless chicken in the oven baked low. I know it is cooked by now. I'll be there in five minutes. I am leaving out now," said Bryant.

"Okay, babe, I am going to get the girls ready for dinner. I'll see you soon. I love you, babe," I said to him before we got off the phone. The phone hung up before he could say I love you back.

The girls and I walked in the house and they ran upstairs as soon as they walked in. I walked in the kitchen. Bryant had the chicken sautéed in garlic and herb sauce. The aroma smelled so good. I walked in the kitchen and turned the oven off. I knew he wanted some vegetables so I grabbed the bag of corn on the cob out of the refrigerator and put them in a pan of water with sea salt, pepper, and butter to let them simmer.

"Babe, what are you doing? I told you I am cooking tonight," Bryant said, walking in the house with a gallon of milk.

"I know, babe, I just wanted to cook the vegetables for you," I said to him.

"Babe, why do you have red lipstick on your lips?" I said to him, as he walked toward me, putting the milk inside the refrigerator.

"I bought some skittles candy from the store being greedy, baby," Bryant said, grabbing a paper towel wiping his lips.

"I am going upstairs to put my pajamas on. When I get back, dinner better be ready," I said to him, smiling and switching, walking up the stairs.

Bryant hit me on the ass, walked into the kitchen, and grabbed another pot for the mashed potatoes. He took the chicken out of the oven and put in on the stove.

His phone vibrated and it was a text message from Michelle saying, *I enjoyed the pleasure. Wink wink.*

Bryant responded back, *don't call me I will call you, baby, I enjoyed it, too*. Then he pressed send.

He turned his cell phone off, walked in the living room to turn to his sports channel which was ESPN football. I walked downstairs, sat beside Bryant, and snuggled with him. He said, "Babe, come on, you know how I get when I am watching my sports."

I gave him a kiss on his neck then went to go check on the food. Everything was done, so I made the girls plates first, then and Bryant's and my plates.

"Girls, come down to eat," I yelled upstairs.

"Okay, Mommy," the girls responded.

Bryant walked toward the dinner table and sat in his favorite chair close to the TV, so he could continue to watch his sports. I sat in the chair across from him. I wanted to ask him who Michelle Humphries was so much that I just blurted it out before the girls came down the stairs.

"Babe, who is Michelle Humphries?"

Bryant almost choked on his wine and said, "Baby, I know you didn't look in my phone again. I thought we been through this already." He gave me a look of guilt and said, "Babe, that's just one of my coworker who does my marketing. I am sorry that she made you feel uncomfortable, you know I love you, baby. I made a promise, remember?"

I looked at him and said, "I hope so, I am not good with disappointments, Bryant."

Aniyah and Eniyah came downstairs and sat at the dinner table. Eniyah was so close to her father, she sat right beside him and Aniyah sat beside me.

"Can we talk about this some other time, babe? I have no reason to lie to you," Bryant said.

"That's fine, babe," I said to him. I said grace over the food and then we all ate as a family.

I put the kids to sleep while Bryant was in the shower. I waited until he got out and approached him about the phone call at the house a couple of months ago.

"Babe, what's up with you and this accusing shit? Why are you fucking starting shit with me? DAMN!" Bryant yelled.

"I am not putting up with these fucking lies, nigga," I said to him.

Bryant walked toward me, grabbed me by my face, and said, "I had enough of this shit with you."

He threw me against the wall, knocking our wedding picture down. I came to him and said, "Don't you ever put your hands on me." Bryant then took his fist and stole the dog shit out of me like I was a man on the street. I fell to the ground crying, holding my face.

He looked at me and said, "Look what you made me do." Then, he walked toward his closet, put his black Roca Wear sweat hoodie on, and grabbed his dark denim blue jeans and his New Balance tennis shoes, grabbed his car keys, and left out of the house.

I was so emotional that I picked up our married picture frame, which was cracked, and threw it against the wall. The person I had on my mind was Saniyah. I rang her phone twice and she finally picked up. I cried on the phone telling her word for word what happened. She offered to come over to the house and I told her no, I just wanted her advice.

"Jocelyn, I will talk to him. Just calm down, both of you all are upset right now and you can't keep accusing that man, he loves you," she said.

"You don't understand, Saniyah, it's too much evidence. He already cheated. What makes you think he won't cheat again? As soon as I catch him, this marriage is over and he will pay," I said to her.

Tears begin to roll down my face and my nose was running. My face was so swollen up that I told her that I would call her later. I hurried downstairs while the girls were asleep. I got in my car and drove to the nearest police station to press charges on him. Once I got in the police station, the officer noticed my swollen face and busted lip and asked me if I needed to get to the hospital. I shook my head no and said, "I would like to file charges on Mr. Bryant Carter and get a stay away order on him, if possible.

The police office looked at me and said, "Are you sure?"

I filed charges and sat down at the table with the office who asked me a bunch of questions. All types of thoughts were running through my head. He stated to me that I would have to go to court and testify. I didn't care. I was angry and this would teach Bryant a lesson to not put his hands on me again. I took the paperwork and walked out of the station. The girls were left at home by themselves and I didn't know who else to turn to. Bryant had never been so upset like this before. Once I left the police station, I drove home, doing 70 mph. I arrived at home in 15 minutes. I called Bryant's phone and it rang and rang, and then went to voicemail. I knew he wasn't coming back for a while and I needed to get in the shower. I went to check on the girls, they were sleep. I cleaned up the glass from the broken picture frame, walked into the bathroom, turned the bath water on, and took a hot bubble bath.

I was upset and depressed at this point. I sat in that bath for almost an hour. When I got out, I thought about calling Bryant's cell phone but I didn't know why I should. *He hit me*, I thought to myself. I prayed, got in my comfortable bed, and went to sleep.

Meeting Victoria
Chapter 8

"We need to talk,"Saniyah said to Bryant, calling his cell phone.

"About what?" he replied back.

"It's been two weeks and you and Jocelyn still haven't spoken to each other. What's going on with you both? You have kids together. Meet me at the park," Saniyah said.

Bryant left the office on his lunch break to meet Saniyah at the park. Saniyah was there working out, doing her weekly Tuesday routine, exercising and listening to her iPod. She gave him a hug once she saw him and they both walked toward the bench to sit down.

"You need to apologize to your wife, she loves you so much. Start by buying her some roses and taking her out to dinner," Saniyah said.

"She is a fucking stubborn bitch, Saniyah. I will try to; she just makes me so mad. Anyway, what's up with you, how you been? I heard you are stepping your game up at the shop. Jocelyn doesn't really have to be there. Congrats to you, Shorty," said Bryant.

"Thanks, babe, but I really need you to apologize and step up to be a man," Saniyah said. She put her hands on his thigh and said, "Life is too short to hold grudges. I love both of you all," she said to him, looking him in his eyes with her long, curly eye lashes.

"I know. Will do. I got to go back to work. I'm on my lunch break." He looked at his watch and said, "Call me later." Then, he got up and walked to his car. Saniyah waved goodbye, put her earplugs back in her ears, and began jogging down the street. Bryant got into his car and called Edible Arrangements to order a fruit basket and a dozen red roses to have them delivered at 7:00p.m.to his address.

I picked the girls up from their after-school program and went to the city mall to pick them up a couple of dresses from JC Penney for church on Sunday. I saw this bad outfit. It was a jean jumper that had silver buttons that met up to my cleavage and I had to buy it. I was tired of sitting in the house, so I made a phone call to Saniyah at least three times before she picked up.

"Okay, we need to get out of the house tonight. I am tired of not doing anything while Bryant pretty much does what the hell he wants to do," I said to her.

"Girl, give it one more day. I have to study tonight. I am trying to get my real estate license, so, sorry, I can't go out tonight," Saniyah replied.

"Mommy, look at this pretty dress, I want it," said Eniyah.

"Girl, I have to go, we are in JC Penney. I had to buy the girls some dresses for church. We all need some prayer in our lives. I will talk to you later. I love you, girl," I said to Saniyah.

"Me, too, sis. I love you, too, talk to you later," Saniyah said before she hung the phone up.

I grabbed my dark blue, jean jumper and grabbed this pretty violet and pink dress with sequins on it for the girls.

We all walked to the shoe department to see if I could buy some BCBG sandals to match the jumper. My phone vibrated and it was Bryant, sending a text message that said he was sorry. I missed his soft, chocolate skin on my body and his soft lips and body heat from us lying in the bed together every night. Bryant had been sleeping on the couch for two weeks since we had the argument. There were times that he didn't even come home. I saw these black, cute sandals that had a sequined strap wrapped around the ankle. I had to get them. I asked the lady that worked at the shoe department for a size eight. She looked at the box and shook her head no, so I asked her if she had any more sizes. She said a size eight-and-a-half. I shook my head and said I will take them. I hurried up and grabbed the box and walked to the cash register and the total came up to $132. I reached down in my Christian Dior bag, searching for my credit card that I could not find. I was holding up the line, but the lady that was behind me was so nice that she offered to pay for it. I said no because my pride wouldn't let me do it!

She said, "Ma'am, I insist. The girls looked at me so sadly and I knew they wanted those dresses. The lady told the woman at the register to add the order to her total. She laid her two shirts on the counter and the woman rung the total up.

"Again, that will be a $198.62."

The lady reached down in her wallet and paid for it with her Discover credit card. I thanked the lady over and over again and I even offered to do her hair at no cost. I asked for her name and she said it was Victoria Lanay Walker.

She gave me her business card and said, "Anytime."

I gave her a big hug and as I was walking toward the front entrance leaving out of the mall, I read the card and it said *Victoria Lanay Walker,* a research lab technician at the Clinical Research of Atlanta.

I said to myself, *this woman works at a research lab, wow,* while walking toward the car. I drove up at the house and my phone vibrated again showing a text that said, *"Where are you"?*

After driving for 35 minutes, I finally drove up to my drive way. Bryant's car was parked in the garage. I got the girls out of the car and grabbed the bags. When attempted to walk up, I noticed an Edible card at the front door. I opened the door, walked toward the kitchen, and saw the beautiful arrangements on the kitchen counter. *What was Bryant up to?* I smiled and tears rolled down my face. It had been a long time since Bryant had been romantic.

The girls walked into the kitchen, holding me by my leg. "Mommy, that's pretty. Did daddy buy you that?" said Aniyah.

"I sure did," Bryant said, walking in the kitchen. He gave me a big hug and kissed me for about 15 seconds. The girls looked at both of us and then ran upstairs to their room. "I know I said this over and over again, but I am very sorry for putting my hands on you. I promise on my life and soul that it will never happen again," he said, as tears rolled down his face. I had never seen Bryant cry, but I was so glad to have my husband back that there wasn't anybody else in this world that could have satisfied me other than him.

"I know, baby, all this for me," I said to him. My eyes were so watery that I had to wipe them twice. I could not stop the tears from coming down my face. Bryant gave me a kiss and walked upstairs to the room. I knew what that meant. I opened the refrigerator door and grabbed two Banquet TV dinners for the girls, put them in the microwave, and waited four minutes until they were ready. I yelled their name, grabbed both of the TV dinners from the microwave, and walked toward their room door.

"Dinner is ready, mommy's babies."

Bryant was in there with them looking at the new dresses I bought them.

"So pretty. Daddy's babies so pretty," he said to them and gave them a big hug and kiss, and walked out of the room, toward our bedroom. I put their food on their Dora the Explorer table, and walked downstairs, to grab some newspaper.

"Enjoy," I said to them, while closing their door.

"We will, Mommy," Aniyah said.

I walked in the bedroom and Bryant was naked under the covers. Candles were lit everywhere. He took the comforter from over the top of his naked body and showed his pretty penis to me. Bryant's cock was so long and big any woman would have loved his pleasure. He was teasing me, jerking his hard shaft up and down. I could not resist him. I took my shirt off, wearing only my black bra, and then I took off my black slacks, showing my lace black underwear.

I walked toward the bed. Bryant got up and grabbed me from the front of my stomach, kissing my belly button and licking me round and round. He started taking my bra off and nibbling on my breasts. I was so horny for my husband that it was like making love to him for the very first time. He laid my body on the bed, still sucking my breasts. He took my panties off and stuck his two fingers inside my wet pussy, fingering me with his long fingers and playing with my clitoris. I begin to moan, sucking on his other fingers.

He inserted himself in me, nice and slow, and we made passionate love for an hour, switching positions. Bryant went to sleep and I slipped on my leopard rope to check on the girls. When I opened their room door, they were asleep. They always slept together even though they had separate twin beds. Eniyah never like sleeping alone. She wanted to be up under her sister. I turned their light off, grabbed the empty TV dinner trays, and walked downstairs to cut the alarm on. I was tired. Bryant had worn me out. When I walked upstairs, I took the business card that Victoria gave me and laid it on the night stand. Then I turned Bryant's side of the light off.

I grabbed one of my favorite books that I like to read by ZANE, Addicted. Ooh, how I was addicted to Bryant even if he was a piece of work. I didn't care, I kissed him on his forehead, read a couple of chapters, and then I dozed off to sleep with the book on my stomach.

Going Through Some Changes Chapter 9

"Victoria, hello, this is Jocelyn. I met you in the JC Penney last month, you probably don't remember me," I said.

"I was waiting for you to call me, hello, dear," Victoria replied.

"I wanted to go to IHOP for brunch. Are you busy?" I asked her.

"No, I am off today, but I was going to stop by the lab to pick something up later. What time are you talking?" Victoria said.

"Meet me at 2741 Claremont Rd, NE Atlanta, GA in an hour," I said, before I hung the phone up.

"See you then," Victoria said, and then we both hung the phone up.

I got dressed fast. I hopped in the shower, lotioned down, and put on my light blue jeans, red tank top, and flat, red shoes with my silver accessories.

I looked so good in my clothes. I was wearing a size 8 just like I was before I had the twins. My schedule was consistent every week, taking the girls to singing practice on Tuesday and dance class on Thursday. I had to keep myself motivated because I was home a lot. Bryant didn't want me to work anymore. Saniyah was taking care of the shop and was now a real estate agent. Everything was working out great.

Traffic was smooth. It was a 30-minute drive from my house, but I got there with no hesitation. Victoria was sitting by the window wearing all black. She was strange to me. She had a wrap on her hair, but her makeup was so fierce. How could I ask this lady to do her hair without offending her? She didn't wear jewelry and was so natural.

"Victoria, we meet again," I said to her, walking toward her, smiling. "I had to meet you and buy you breakfast. Every time I called you, your phone went to voice mail."

She smiled and said, "I know, I was just waiting for this day to come," she looked at me very strangely. "So, Jocelyn, you have a look on you that you are not as happy as your smiles seemed to be. How come? What's bothering you my, dear," she said to me, as if she was a psychic or something.

I sat down across from her and said, "Victoria, I am happily married. Happy. See my ring?"I showed her my cluster wedding ring and smiled and said, "He loves me so much, Victoria, I would do anything to make him happy."

"Jocelyn, I once was married, too. I am a widow now. My husband passed away twenty-five years ago. I am an old lady. I am 52 years old. I never once looked back. I don't have any kids like you so, when I saw those dresses, it reminded me of when I was a little girl and my mom would dress me up for church every Sunday."

The waitress came over to take our orders. I ordered the egg omelet with an orange juice and Victoria ordered a coffee with eggs, no cheese, and potatoes, no meat. She was a vegetarian.

"How did you get to work at a research lab, Victoria?" I asked.

"I got my degree in college. That was my field. I loved to work in the labs, Jocelyn," she said.

"Yes, ma'am," I replied.

"Is your husband faithful to you?" she asks.

"I am not comfortable answering that question. What made you ask me that, Victoria?"

"I see that strange mark on your arm. Are you being abused at home?" she said.

"No, my arm hit a piece of glass on my wall, a picture frame. This happened awhile back. I'm okay. Victoria, I want to share something with you. No, everything is not fine at home. One minute, I forgive him. The next minute, I am always thinking he is cheating on me," I said to her.

The waitress brought the food to the table. "Here is your omelet and orange juice, and here is your eggs, no cheese and potatoes, with your coffee, along with cream and sugar."

"I don't need cream or sugar. I drink my coffee plain, but thanks, anyway," said Victoria. "Jocelyn, can I share a secret with you?" said Victoria, as she sipped her hot, steaming coffee. "I killed my husband."

I looked at her in shock. "Jocelyn, don't be afraid, it was self-defense. At least, that's what I told them," she said. "I was faithful to my husband and he cheated on me and sometimes, beat on me. The police never wanted to get involved because he was a police officer, a fucking officer of the law. Anyway, one night, coming home, I spotted his car in the driveway. He thought I was out of town on business because that's what I told him. I drove up in my drive way, opened the door, and walked upstairs. He was nowhere to be found. I yelled his name three times, but there was no answer.

The red button was beeping on the voicemail, so I checked the voicemail. A woman voice said, "Baby, I am on my way there to pick you up, be ready."

Beep.

I knew that voice. It was Judy that worked for him. She was his personal secretary.

I searched and searched my house for any evidence that might tell me where he was at. She must have called him on his cell phone because he never checked the home voice mail. I looked on the kitchen countertop and saw a pen that read Hilton Suites Hotel. Something stuck in my head. I thought the only Hilton Suites Hotel in this area was on Sullivan Road so I didn't panic or attempt to call him. I left calmly, went upstairs, and grabbed me a pair of clothes and walked out of the house. I wanted to smoke so bad, I lit me two cigarettes to calm my nerves and smoked them at the same time.

I drove an hour away to the lab and grabbed a glass with a top of some sulfuric acid locked up in the cabinet safe and got in my car and drove until I got to the Hilton Suites Hotel. I walked inside with the tall glass of acid, the size to fit inside my big purse, walked toward the front and told the concierge that I was locked out of my room. I stated to him that I had just arrived with Kenneth Vernon Walker. We checked in two hours ago. The concierge typed his name up in the computer and, what a surprise, it pulled right up. "I just need proof of ID, Mrs.

Walker," he said to me, as I showed him my ID, looked at the picture and gave me the room keycard to room 609. I walked toward the elevator and a tall, pretty, blonde-haired woman walked from out of the elevator wearing a black trench coat and red, sexy pump heels. I looked at her up and down, wearing my classy, tinted black shades. I took out of my purse and put on my black, leather gloves and got on the elevator and pressed number six to get on the 6th floor. When I got off the elevator, I immediately walked to my left and made a quick turn to room 609.As I proceeded to walk toward the front door, I heard music coming from out of the room.

I opened the door with my key card slowly. I noticed Kenneth was not there. I tiptoed in and closed the door quietly and checked each part of the room. I heard the water running from the shower. I wanted to catch Kenneth in the act. The smell of sex was in the air and I knew he was in there with a woman. I was going to kill them both. When I opened the bathroom door, I saw a pair of black thongs on the bathroom floor and Kenneth was taking a hot, steaming shower.

His back was turned. As I looked at him washing his face with his rag, he didn't even see me coming. I pulled out my tall bottle of sulfuric acid and untwisted the top open and slid open the shower door. I turned the shower water off and Kenneth looked at me with a surprise. "What are you doing here?" he yelled. I responded, "I am here for you, babe." I threw the acid in Kenneth's face and watched his face sizzle. He yelled and tried to get out of the shower but kept slipping. I threw some more acid on him until it was all gone. Kenneth fell in the shower and hit his head on the soap holder. Blood was gushing out of his head; he was knocked out unconscious, and died instantly. I picked up the pair of black panties and left out of the bathroom, threw the panties on the bed, and left out of the room.

I walked toward the elevator and took the gloves off and put them in the trash can next to the elevators, took my wig off and the jacket I wore in there, got on the elevator and pressed L for lobby. When the elevator stopped, I looked to see if the concierge was still there. He was too busy on the computer, so I walked past him and barely notice he said, "Have a great night." I answered disguising my voice, "You do the same," and walked out like I was the Queen Bitch of New York."

"Damn, you got balls," I said to Victoria, as she looked at me.

"Jocelyn, it's not about having balls. What makes you weak will only make you stronger. Think about our conversation today and take heed to it before it's too late," Victoria said to me. She got up from the table and, before she walked away, she said, "Call me so we can hook up some other time." Then she left out of the café. I was so scared. All types of thoughts were running in my head. This lady just told me she killed her husband a couple of years ago and didn't get any jail time for it. Why was she giving me this type of advice? I could never kill Bryant. I loved him too much for that, but the question I said to myself, is *does Bryant love me*?

"Saniyah, what are you doing here? I thought you didn't believe in all that sex toy crap," Bryant said to Saniyah.

"Whom? The question is, what are you doing here? It better be for Jocelyn," Saniyah said to him.

"Who else, Saniyah? My wife got me in here buying her some handcuffs and motion lotion. You know that girl is freaky," said Bryant.

Saniyah walked up to him and said, "what about you, Bryant, are you freaky, too?"

As she walked to the cash register and asked the girl who worked at the store for some anal ease, the girl asked her which flavor she would like. She responded cherry, of course. Bryant looked at Saniyah with a seductive look. He was so weak for pretty, light-skinned women and he always had a fantasy of her and Jocelyn together giving him foreplay. Saniyah attempted to walk out of the door, but Bryant grabbed her by the arms and said, "Saniyah, we need to talk. Why don't you meet me somewhere in 10minutes?"

"Where?"Saniyah replied.

"Meet you where? Why don't we meet at your house?" Bryant said, "And catches up on some things before I dropped these items off to Jocelyn."

"Cool," Saniyah said. "Let's roll."

Bryant walked back to the cash register. "I am sorry, I forgot to pay for these items," he said to the young girl.

She looked at him and said, "No problem, handsome, you could have used them on me." Then she smiled at him. Bryant paid for the items with his Visa credit card, signed the receipt, and then left out of the store.

He walked toward Saniyah and asked her, "What you meant when you said I was freaky, too."

"I didn't mean it that way, silly." She smiled at him and then they both walked toward their cars. Saniyah started her new 2000 silver Denali truck and drove off. Bryant followed her in his Benz, driving for about 30minutes. They drove up in front of Saniyah's house and Saniyah parked her car inside of her garage. Bryant pulled up behind her truck. She got out of her truck and opened the door to her town house where she lived by herself with her dog, Jack. Bryant walked in from behind her, watching her ass jiggle in her tight leggings. She walked in the kitchen and bent over to give her puppy something to eat.

"Can I offer you anything to drink? I have Remy, Vodka, Hennessey, and Jack Daniels over there at the bar. Go pour your trouble."

"Will do. It isn't like I have not been here before," Bryant said, smiling at Saniyah.

"I know, nigga," she replied, "This is your home, too."

"Do you want a glass of anything?" Bryant said to her.

"I sure do. Please pour me some Remy on the rocks. The ice is located in the cooler at the bottom of the bar mini refrigerator."

He poured us both some Remy on rocks and walked to the couch. Saniyah walked toward him and said, "So, tell me, what's been going on with you and Jocelyn? I have not talked to her in a week. I have been busy doing my real estate thing. I know she is back and forth at the shop, so, what's good?"

"Business is doing very good for both of us, very good." He took a big sip of his Remy and said, "enough about us, Saniyah, can I tell you something?"

"Sure, Bryant," she said.

"I caught Jocelyn cheating on me with Mike. I never told anybody but you, so you makes sure you keep this a secret. They were fucking on my couch one night about a month ago.

I came home and they didn't notice I was there watching them. I left out without making a sound. Jocelyn was moaning like she didn't care if I saw her or not and he was pounding her from behind, gripping her ass. You are the only person I can talk to about this so, please, don't tell anybody else. Don't even bring it up to Jocelyn or Mike."

Bryant laid his head in Saniyah lap and acted like he was crying. "I love her, why would she cheat on me with my best friend?" He made a soft crying sound and started sniffling.

Saniyah said, "Well, Bryant, I think you should do the same thing in return."

He looked up at her and put his hand under her shirt, massaging her breasts. He started kissing her stomach, licking her belly button. Saniyah opened her legs and put her fingers through Bryant curly hair. He sucked her stomach then started sucking her breasts. She took her shirt off then pulled her leggings down. He took her underwear off then they started tongue kissing.

Bryant's cock was so hard that he couldn't wait to thrust her pussy. She took out his large cock from out of his pants and started massaging his shaft up and down, taking his pants down to his ankles. He laid her back on the couch. Saniyah wanted him to insert her from behind. She grabbed the anal ease from out of her purse on the end table from the couch and gave it to him. He took her underwear off and bent her over, showing her red, round ass. He put some anal ease on his two fingers and stuck his two fingers in her ass. She moaned out loud and then he put some anal ease on his throbbing cock and inserted it inside her slowly, with only the tip of his cock. She wanted him to go deep, so he went deep inside her anus, in and out. Saniyah eyes were so big. She enjoyed all of him. He put her hands behind her and pounded her hard, then harder, nonstop. She loved every bit of it. She took control and rocked back and forth on his cock nonstop until he was all the way in there. Bryant moaned out so loud he said, "DAMN, Saniyah, your ass is so good and open and so wet. He took his cock out and then put it inside her wet canal. He grabbed her hair, and then grabbed her shoulders, pounding her doggy-style from behind.

"You like this good cock, don't you?"

"Yes, baby, I do," she replied and moaned, then moaned again. She took control again, got up from her position, and sat him on the couch. She got on top of him and started riding his cock with her ass facing toward him. He pounded her asshole thrashing, in and out, up and down, while he was holding her small waist. She played with her clitoris while riding him. Bryant moaned out loud and they both climax at the same time.

His cell phone rang three times, and then vibrated. "Shit, I got to go. Let me wash up a little," he said to her. "I need a wash cloth," he asked her.

She replied, “their down the hallway in the linen closet, beside the bathroom,” pointing in the direction of the bathroom.

He hurried up and walked that direction, grabbed a wash cloth, and proceeded to walk to the bathroom. Bryant felt guilty, but also enjoyed the pleasure from Saniyah. She had him hooked. He knew he had to go home and make love to Jocelyn, but also knew Saniyah was going to be on his mind. Bryant left out of the bathroom and walked toward the couch to grab his cell phone from the end table. “I got to go, Saniyah,” he said to her and kissed her on her forehead.

She walked him to the door naked before she opened it. He grabbed her face and began tongue kissing her gently. Then he opened the door and left out. Saniyah shut the door, went upstairs and turned the shower water on to take her a steaming, hot shower.

Bryant opened his car door. He noticed that Saniyah’s nosy neighbor was waving bye to him but he waved back and drove off quickly. His cell phone rang again.

“I am on my way home, babe. I wasn’t ignoring your call; I just had to meet Mike somewhere. It was an emergency,” he said to her.

I didn’t even bother to ask him questions, I just simply said, “okay, baby, just make it home safely. The kids are worried about you. We have not seen you since this morning. When I came home, you were gone.”

“I know, baby, you always told me if friends needed help, we are always supposed to help them, no matter what, right,” he replied back.

"Okay, babe, I'll see you when you get home," I said to him, and then I hung up.

Speaking of friends, I decided to call Saniyah. I had not heard from her going on two weeks.

Ring Ring Ring

There was no answer, so I hung up and called her home phone.

Ring Ring

"Hello,"Saniyah said.

"Hey, girl, what's up? It's me," I said to her.

"Hey, girl, I was just laying down. What's up?" Saniyah said.

"Nothing, just checking up on you. I wanted to come see you tomorrow if that's okay with you," I said to her.

"Anytime, Jocelyn, you know I don't mind. What time so I can prepare you your favorite dish, herb and garlic chicken with brown rice," Saniyah said to me.

"Around 4:30, if that's fine with you."

"Sounds like a plan. I can't wait," Saniyah said.

"Okay, see you then. I love you, babe," I said to her. Just before we were getting ready to hang the phone up, Bryant walked in from the front door and gave me a kiss on my forehead, then walked toward the kitchen and asked what was for dinner. "I have to go, Saniyah, let me tend to my husband, he just walked in and said hello."

"Tell him I said hello, too, I got to go, Jocelyn. I will see you tomorrow."

"I will see you tomorrow, too, Saniyah."

"Saniyah said hello, Bryant."He asked me where I was going tomorrow.

I replied, "Just over Saniyah's house. We have a dinner date, just me and her. Best friends for life."

"Sounds boring. Where are my girls?" Bryant asks me.

"They are sound asleep. They had them two biscuits apiece and I fixed them a can of Ravioli in tomato sauce. They ate that and went to bed early."

Bryant fixed him a sandwich, with chips and poured him some orange juice.

The conversation was short between us. He grabbed his food, walked toward the stairs, and said, "Baby, I am going to eat my food then get in the shower and go to bed. I have an early meeting tomorrow with staff about the proposals for the new restaurant we are trying to buy and I can't be late. You don't mind, do you?" he asked as he proceeded to walk up the stairs.

I shook my head and said, "no, but, Bryant, I thought we were using our sex toys tonight."

He ignored me and proceeded to walk up the stairs. I propped my feet up on the couch, grabbed my laptop, and read my messages from my yahoo account. As I was scrolling through my messages, I stopped at this one message from Mrs. Victoria Walker.

I opened the message and it read: *It's not too late. He may have gotten your heart, but don't let him get your mind. Move forward and live your life. Don't let nothing get in your way from making your decisions, if you know what I mean.* I quickly clicked out of the message and slammed my laptop. All kinds of thoughts were running through my head. I knew Bryant was still cheating, but I couldn't lay my finger on it. Victoria was like an angel who was giving me signs and I couldn't let her down. I wanted to give her a call ASAP, but it wasn't a good time because Bryant was there. I put my laptop away, grabbed the remote to the TV, and started watching my Lifetime channel. After an hour went by, I fell asleep quickly.

Scandalous Hoes
Chapter 10

I drove up in front of Saniyah's house around 4:30p.m.the next day and her nosy ass neighbor, Mrs. Kindle, kept waving at me. She then waved at me to come her direction. I parked my car, got out, and walked toward her. "Yes, ma'am, can I help you?"

"Jocelyn, I have not seen you in forever. Where have you been?" Mrs. Kindle said.

"Working and being a mom, taking care of the twins, that's all, Mrs. Kindle."

"That man you married to-what's his name?" she asked.

"Who? Bryant?"

"Yes, that's his name. I saw him yesterday over here with your girlfriend, Saniyah. I saw him when he was driving out of her drive way. He is so nice, he waved goodbye to me."

"Oh, really? That's strange, Mrs. Kindle, are you sure that was Bryant? He wasn't in this area yesterday," I said to her, giving her a strange look.

"Baby, I know I am 63 years old, but these eyes don't fool me one bit," said Mrs. Kindle.

"Well, Mrs. Kindle, it was nice talking to you. I have to see Saniyah. It was nice seeing you again," I said, walking away toward Saniyah's front door.

"Okay, Jocelyn, I hope to see you again," Mrs. Kindle said, walking toward her backyard.

I rung the door bell and Saniyah opened the door and gave me a hug. "Hello, babe, I miss you," she said, smiling.

"I miss you, too," I said to her.

"What's wrong?" Saniyah asked me.

"Ooh, girl, nothing, just had something on my mind. It smells good in here," I said to her.

"Your herb garlic chicken you requested, remember," Saniyah said.

"I need a drink. It's been stressful for me. What you got, girl?" I asked.

"Your favorite, Remy VSOP. You know where to go and get it, nothing's changed around here, girl," Saniyah said, pointing to the direction of the bar.

I walked toward the bar, grabbed me a glass, and walked toward the freezer to grab two ice cubes from the ice tray. My phone ranged and it was Bryant.

"Hey, baby. I got the girls. Where are you?" he asked.

"Babe, you forget? Me and Saniyah have a dinner date," I said to him.

"Ooh, I forgot, babe, that's right, you did say that you were going to be there today. I miss you," he said.

"I know. I will be home later. You make sure you put the kids to sleep and I will show you that I missed you, too," I said to him.

I was walking toward the couch before I sat down and I noticed Bryant's Armani watch in the corner of the couch.

"Babe, I love you, let me call you back," I said to him and then I hung the phone up. I grabbed the watch and stuck it in my purse.

Saniyah walked in and said, "girl, was that you Prince Charming on the phone?" she smiled.

"You know what, Saniyah; let's make a toast to friendship. Friends that won't lie to each other, friends that love and care about each other," I said.

"Yes, I do agree, Jocelyn," Saniyah said. We toasted our glasses together and took a big sip.

"Let me check on the herb garlic chicken. The brown rice is done and the vegetables need more butter," Saniyah said. She got up from the couch and walked toward the kitchen. I walked to the bar and poured me another glass of REMY VSOP and a little bit of ginger ale.

"Girl, dinner is ready," said Saniyah.

"I am starving," I said.

I walked toward the dining room table, sat down, and Saniyah served me my plate of food. Then she walked in the kitchen and to make her plate and sat across from me at the dinner table.

We both looked at each other eye to eye. I wanted to approach Saniyah so badly about what Mrs. Kindle said and Bryant's watch. I ate some more of my vegetables and a small piece of my chicken.

"So, Saniyah, how's life been treating you? Met anybody lately?" I said to her, wiping my mouth with my napkin.

"No complaints. I have been chilling. I really don't want to be bothered with no DAMN man right now. They are all dogs," she said to me, giving me a strange look.

"Dogs, huh?" I smiled and said, "Ha."

"Yes, girl, you know dog's roof roof," she said to me and smiled.

"Have you talked to Mike lately?" I asked her.

"No, I have not. I have been busy with real estate. Business is looking good for me right now. What about yourself, Jocelyn?"

"Can't complain. I live it day by day, that's all I can say. You know what, look at the time, Saniyah, I have to go and make sure the girls clothes are ironed for tomorrow," I said.

I got up from the seat, put my plate in the sink, grabbed my glass of Remy, took a big sip, and walked toward Saniyah and took a look at her while she was eating her food. I kissed her on her cheek and left out of the house.

My mind was so confused. My heart was in pain. I wanted so bad to bring it to Bryant's attention. I stopped the car at this stop sign and prayed to God to give me the strength not to go to jail and hurt somebody. When I pulled in my drive way, my lights were turned on in my bedroom. I turned the car off, walked in my house, closed the door, and walked to the girls' room to check on them. They were sound asleep. Bryant was a great father and loved his girls no matter what. He even had their clothes ironed and hung up for school the next day.

I walked in the bedroom and noticed the smell of vanilla candles lit throughout the room. Bryant had soft music playing and had laid my satin night gown out on the bed with a white thong and my white satin bra. I just could not believe him. I wanted to approach him so badly, but after I saw how he had the room smelling good, candles lit, all of my anger went out of the door.

Bryant knew I was so weak for his chocolate. He came out of the shower with his six-pack showing and nothing else on. His cock was rock-hard as if he smelled my scent coming home.

"Baby, come here," he said to me.

I walked toward him with no hesitation. He grabbed my plump ass and gently took off my shirt and pants. Then, he sat me on the bed and took my sandals off.

Wearing only my bra and underwear, Bryant undressed me, put on my satin robe, and laid me on the bed, kissing every body part you can name. He turned the lamp lights off and we began making love.

"Babe, I'll see you later. I have to go out of town for a conference in Los Angeles. We are having our grand opening at one of the restaurants."

"No problem, Bryant, I will see you when you get home, babe, have a safe trip."

"Kiss the girls for me, I have to catch this flight," said Bryant. "I will call you when I get there." He kissed me on my forehead and left out the room. I glanced at the clock it said 5:38 a.m.

I didn't question Bryant. At this point, I really didn't care. I jumped out of bed, turned the hot water on, and got in the steaming, hot shower. As tears rolled down my face, I began to break down for some reason. I didn't trust him anymore. Victoria was on my mind. I had to meet her again to get some advice. The girls needed to be in school in two hours, so I washed my body all over, got out of the shower, and towel-dried myself.

Where's my laptop? I said to myself. I grabbed it from the closet and sent Victoria a message. I lotioned my body down with Shea butter, walked toward the girls' bedroom, and woke them up for school. I walked back into my room and put on my ashy pair of jeans and white fitted T-shirt with my white Nikes, and grabbed my fitted blue cap.

The girls brushed their teeth, washed their faces, and took their scarves off of their long, curly hair. Victoria replied back asking where I wanted to meet. I replied back and stated that I wanted to meet at the café-the same place we met last. She replied back and said, *let's meet in an hour.* Cool. I closed my laptop, grabbed the girls to walk them downstairs, and left out of the house, putting the code into the alarm.

We all got in the car and then I drove off. After driving for about ten minutes, I arrived at their school. The girls were so happy.

"Bye, Mom," they said and gave me a big kiss on the cheek. They both opened the door and ran toward the school door. I waited and watched them go into the school building, and then I pulled off. I arrived at the café in 30minutes. Victoria was sitting at the same table we sat before, drinking her dark coffee and eating her wheat toast bread.

"I'm sorry that I ordered before you," said Victoria.

"No problem; I am not hungry."

"What's wrong, my dear? What's the rush to see me? Did you change your mind?" said Victoria.

"I have a lot on my plate, Victoria," I said to her.

"I am not happy. Bryant's cheating is getting worse, I feel it," I said to her.

"Can you prove it?" Jocelyn she said to me, giving me a strange look and sipping her coffee.

"No, but I will catch him and when I do, it's not going to be a pretty picture," I said to her, looking very angry.

"Jocelyn, how many times I told you? Better do it now before it's too late," said Victoria.

"You know, Victoria, I found his watch in my best friend's couch. Then, her neighbor told me that she saw him the day before. Who should I believe?" I said to her.

"God, Jocelyn, that's the only person you can trust right now."

I believed anything that Victoria said to me. She handed me a gift bag with a very large glass bottle that had acid in it. The bag was so heavy. She said that she wanted me to be happy and that this will make it all better. I grabbed the large gift bag and got up to leave. Victoria smiled at me and said, "You will know when it is the right time."

I didn't even say goodbye. Emotions started to take over. I probably would have thrown the acid in Bryant's face in front of everybody. I was so depressed that tears kept running down my face. I didn't want to bring it up to Saniyah because I knew Bryant would not do that to me. Not in a lifetime; he loved me too much. But,

Saniyah, she would just lie to me with a sneaky smile on her face.

"Babe, I finally made it here and I am exhausted from the plane ride," he said to me.

"I know, baby. I know you are tired, so get you some rest. I am on my way to the gym for an hour, and then come back here to take the girls to the movies later," I said to him.

"Kiss my babies for me," said Bryant. "Muah, I love you, babe, I have to talk to you later. I am getting ready to take a shower and relax." We both hung the phone up and kissed each other over the phone.

"I thought you would never get off the phone," Cindy said to him, seductively lying across her king-sized, heart-shaped bed.

Bryant walked toward Cindy, laid beside her, and begins kissing her lips gently. As he kissed her soft lips, he began to unsnap her bra. "I miss you, baby, I have been waiting for a whole year for this," she whispered in his ear.

"I know, baby, I know," he responded, while getting on top of her.

They began making love nonstop.

"Now, you know it's been a long time, Jocelyn, you have to work those abs and hamstrings. Come on, give me 10 more," my personal trainer yelled.

I said, "10 more."I was so tired I had to catch my breath. I was also lonely and gullible, wanting attention from any man. I was fit, but lost 10 pounds from what you call stress. I really needed to exercise because I had a lot on my mind with Bryant, Saniyah, and Victoria. What could possible go wrong now?

Bryant was in Chicago? *Should I go take a flight and surprise him?* I stopped exercising, grabbed the girls from the daycare facility, grabbed my gym bag, and proceeded to walk toward my car.

"You girls want some McDonald's?" I ask them. I drove to the nearest McDonald's, got two happy meals with apple juice, parked in front of a liquor store, and purchased a bottle of Vodka with cranberry juice.

I was so overwhelmed at this point. I didn't know who to turn to, so, as soon as I and the girls drove up to the house, I parked the car quickly and opened the door. The girls ran upstairs to eat their food. I checked my voicemail to see if I had any missed calls and something dawned on me that I needed to call my mom. I put my purse and gym bag down on the dining room table and called my mom.

Ring Ring Ring

"Hello," she said in her soft voice."

"Mom, I miss you," I said to her.

"Baby, thanks for checking on me. I was lying down. When are my girls coming to visit me? Why don't you send them here to keep me company?"

"You know what, Mom, I might just do that," I said.

"What's wrong, Jocelyn? I hear it in your voice. Are you okay?" she said to me.

"Yes, Mom, I am okay, just taking it day by day."

I began pouring myself a glass of Vodka and cranberry juice. "Mom, I have to tell you something," I said to her.

"What's wrong, Jocelyn," she asked.

"Well, I…Mom, I am not happy with Bryant and I don't know why I have a feeling about things. I maybe just need to go back to work and stop being home. Bryant is stressing me out. I have not been to work in months, Mom."

"What you mean, Jocelyn? Bryant is a good man, why assume such a thing?" she said.

"Never mind, Mom, you right. Bryant is a good husband at times," I said to her.

"Baby, you have to trust your husband. He is providing for you and the girls and I know you love him. Let a man be a man and step back and let him wear the pants, Jocelyn."

"Mom, I know, but what now? He is out town and I am here. He didn't ask if I wanted to go and I know deep down in my heart, that it is strictly business, I know this, but, Mom, when I was laying in that hospital bed, Bryant promised me that he would never hurt me again and that he loved my unconditionally."

"And that's why I am telling you he loves you, Jocelyn. No need to worry. God is going to work it out for you Marilyn said.

"Okay, Mom, I love you. I have to go. I will call you tomorrow so I can send the girls to come visit you next month. I have to wait until Bryant gets back from Chicago. I got to go now. I love you. Muah." I kissed the phone and then hung up.

I guzzled that glass of Vodka down, walked toward the living room and put on some music. I was so depressed at this point. I wanted to just go in the mirror, grab a knife, and cut myself. I didn't feel attractive anymore so I looked at myself in my large mirror by the entertainment system and cried. I cried and really cried. I was so heartbroken but didn't know what the real reason was. I knew I couldn't trust Bryant because he cheated on me before. What makes him so different now?

I wished I would have died in the hospital. I was so miserable. I grabbed my cell phone, waiting for my husband to call me. I rang his phone twice and there was no answer. I knew he was in a meeting and I didn't want to disturb him. So, I hung the phone up and called him again. Still no answer. I left a message and just before I could speak, the phone beeped in.

"Hey, baby, what's wrong? I couldn't answer my phone because we are in a conference call meeting," Bryant said.

"Baby, I don't think I can do this anymore," I said to him.

"Do what, Jocelyn," he said to me.

"I want a divorce," I said to him, crying even more on the phone.

"Baby, what are you talking about? You don't believe me or you don't trust me," he asked me.

"Neither one. I am packing my shit and I am going to stay with my mom for a while, me and the girls. So, when you come home, I won't be here," I said to him.

"Baby, have you been drinking?" He asked me where my girls were. He asked me where my girls were?.

"Why are you so fucking worried? You went out of town on us," I yelled back at him.

"Jocelyn, sleep it off, baby, you don't mean that. You got everything you need. Money, cars, jewelry, what else do you want from me, baby, what?" he said.

"You figure it out, Bryant Carter, you fucking figure it out."

I hung the phone up on him and cried on the couch, holding the pillow in my face.

"Is everything okay?" Cindy asked.

"Yes, I am fine, just had to take an important phone call. Are you finished with your dinner?" he asked her.

"Yes, but this place is gorgeous, I don't want to leave. The jazz band is nice and I am enjoying this atmosphere," she said to him, kissing him on his cheek.

"Look, Cindy, I can't do this anymore. I have to leave Friday morning to go check on my girls and their Mom."

"Ooh, you and Jocelyn are still together?" she asks him.

"No, we are not, but that's still my wife and the mother of my kids and right now, I don't want to have this conversation with you. Stop being in my fucking business," he yelled at her, and then got up from the table and left out.

Cindy got up from the dinner table. She was so embarrassed. She ran behind Bryant and they both flagged a taxi down.

"Bryant, I am sorry, baby," she said to him as they both got in the cab. "27 Gallery Place, please," Cindy said to the cab driver.

While heading the direction to Cindy's mansion, Bryant says to her, "I need to be by myself right now. I will see you tomorrow before I go back to Atlanta."

Cindy didn't respond. The cab driver drove up her long drive way to the mansion. Cindy walked out and slammed the door. She looked back to notice the cab driver driving off quickly.

"Please take me to the Hilton Hotel, please," Bryant said to the cab driver aggressively. After driving for 30 minutes, they finally drove up in front of the Hilton Hotel. Bryant thought about calling Jocelyn, but he didn't. He knew she was upset and had a good reason to be upset. Bryant knew he couldn't change his ways. His weakness was loving beautiful women. Opening his room door, he felt lonely. He immediately took his white shirt and black linen slacks off and lies across the bed, thinking of the argument that he and I had.

I awakened, feeling sick. I couldn't believe I drank the whole bottle and cranberry juice. This was not me. I got up to check on the girls and they were still asleep. I checked my phone to see who called. My husband did, but there was no message. It had been a stressful week for me and I needed to relax and get on the plane to go somewhere-anywhere.

I didn't know when Bryant was coming home and I really didn't care. I walked in the bathroom to turn the shower on, took my clothes off, and got right in the warm water. It felt so relaxing to my body. I washed my long hair and my face. I know I was in the shower for at least 30 minutes because Aniyah was knocking on the door.

"Mom, can I have some cereal and milk," she said to me.

"Yes, baby, go ahead. I will be in here for a little while, just need to clear my head a little." Aniyah slammed the door by mistake, ran downstairs to the kitchen, and grabbed two bowls and two spoons. She poured some milk and grabbed her box of Fruit Loops.

Eniyah walked downstairs and said, “hey, what about me?” She smiled, dragged her chair beside Aniyah, grabbed her bowl of cereal, and began eating. They both were staring at the box of cereal and swinging their feet in the chair, humming their favorite song, Jesus Loves Me. I was so emotional. This time was the hardest for me ever. I cried so badly that I just sat in the tub and let the water wet my hair and face.

Pleasure is All Mine
Chapter 11

I hope I packed enough, I said to myself, dragging three suitcases out of the door. Bryant was beeping the horn. "Babe, come on, you are going to miss your flight."

"I'm coming. I have to grab my purse." Jamaica, here I come. I was so relieved that mean Bryant had been going to therapy. Our lives were coming together with no drama. The girls were with my mom. I needed this time to myself. I trust my husband. It's been two months free of stress.

Bryant wanted me to go to Jamaica by myself. He stated that I needed that alone time and I truly agreed. I got in the passenger side of my car and Bryant drove off.

"Babe, please don't mess this opportunity up. Enjoy your vacation time to yourself, Daddy will be home waiting for you," he said to me, giving me full eye contact.

"You make sure you go to the barber shop and get that hair cut off. When I come home, I want all of that hair chopped off your face and your hair well-cut," I said to him, giving him a strange look.

After driving for an hour, we finally drove up to the airport. I was 30 minutes early. I got out of my car and Bryant got out of the driver's side. He helped me with my three suitcases.

"Damn, baby, what did you pack in here? A body?" he said to me, laughing.

"Yep, I packed your dog that died a couple of years ago, ha," I said to him, smiling.

"Babe, that's not funny. I miss Rocky, that was my little homie," he said to me, with a little smirk on his face.

I gave him a big kiss, walked toward the glass doors, and walked to Gate C to weigh my suitcases. Bryant walked to the glass doors and watched me walk through the metal detector.

Ring Ring

His phone rang. "What's up, my nigga?" Mike said.

"Oh, nothing just dropped Jocelyn off to the airport."

"For what? Where she going?" Mike asked.

"Jamaica. Jamaica, where's that good Bob Marley?" Bryant said, smiling over the phone.

"I want to get with you later. Why don't you come to the spot?" Mike said.

"Aw, man, you still is fucking them stripper bitches?" Bryant said.

"And you know this, man," said Mike.

"Ha, I'll be there later. I'll go with you as soon as I get my shape up and haircut at Barber 1," said Bryant.

"Cool, I'll get at you, hit me up," said Mike.

"Will do," Bryant said. He hung the phone up, got in the car, and drove off.

"Nigga, where you been?" said the barber.

"Shit, I been doing my chef thing. Life is looking real good right about now, real good," said Bryant as he walks toward the barber seat.

"Shit, your wife's business been real good across the street. Her girlfriend Saniyah been holding it down," said the barber.

"Yes, I know, that's why she is in Jamaica right now so she can relax and chill," Bryant said.

"Man, you doing big things," said the barber.

"Nope, just living day by day, that's all we can do," said Bryant. "The wife wants the goatee back and the haircut. Love that, shit turns her on," Bryant said.

"I got you, she wants the old Bryant with the wavy hair, huh?" said the barber.

Bryant smiled and said, "Well, you know got to keep her happy." He rubbed his hands together and smiled.

"Man, that Saniyah is phat to death, you need to hook a nigga up," said the barber.

"Man you crazy; ask her-she might let you take her out. I don't have anything to do with that," said Bryant.

Ring RingRing

Bryant's answering machine came on after the beep. I left a message, "hey, baby, I am on the plane. First class is the bomb. Sipping my Remy VSOP and getting ready to turn my iPod on. I love you, call me back ASAP!"

Then I hung the phone up. "Ma'am, did you need anything else?" the flight attended asked.

"No, I am fine, but thanks," I responded.

I was thinking all types of thoughts on what to do in Jamaica. I knew one thing, if I see a Mandingo; he might get it down here. Shit, why not? *If Bryant cheated, why can't I?* I thought to myself. I closed my eyes while playing my iPod and dozed off to sleep, not realizing the cup was still in my hand. It was empty and fell to the floor. I was riding on cloud nine. I had this strange dream where Victoria appeared to me. I dreamed I caught Bryant cheating on me but, for some reason, I couldn't get the picture of the woman.

Bryant was in our bed making love this woman. I could hear the moaning sounds from downstairs and the smell of sex was in the air. I tip-toed up to our bedroom, open the door gently, and watched them make love. Bryant was on top of her like he makes love to me and she was making a soft sound like it felt really good to her.

I called his name, "Bryant."

For some reason, he couldn't hear me. "Bryant," I said again and then I woke up. My heart was beating so fast. I looked at everybody around me on the plane that was asleep. I was so glad that was only a dream and not real.

I closed my eyes. R Kelly's "*When a Woman's Fed Up*" was on repeat. I pushed the button to the next song, closed my eyes and just relaxed. I had three more hours to get to Jamaica. I was excited. This was my second time in Montego Bay and the view of the clear, turquoise water was so beautiful. Everybody that lived there was so nice and friendly. It was nothing like down south ATL which was full of bourgeois women and men that were pretty much fucking spoiled.

Three hours later, which came quickly, we landed at the Sangster International Airport. I couldn't wait to call Bryant. I missed him and the kids. Once the plane stopped and the flight attendant gave us instructions, I grabbed my carryon luggage and big Louis Vuitton duffle bag, and proceeded to walk toward the ramp toward the airport to get to the Sandals Lounge to wait for the shuttle bus to drive me to the resort which was 15 minutes away from the airport.

I waited five minutes and the shuttle bus arrived in seconds. We arrived at Sandals to my suite called Bay Roc Estate. It was gorgeous! This was something different from where Bryant and I stayed. I love Sandals of Montego Bay. My first time here was for Bryant's and my honeymoon. The resort was all inclusive with unlimited dining and drinking. It had seven restaurants, five different kinds of bars and four pools. The beach stretched a long way and the white sand was so soft you could sink your feet right in. I had a beautiful beach front suite. I quickly wanted to get in the shower. I felt sluggish from the plane ride. I received a text from Bryant saying that he loves me and he wants me to give him a call ASAP. I had a nice, king-sized bed all to myself. I walked around, took out my digital camera, and took pictures of every part of the room-the expansive marble-finished bathrooms, Jacuzzi tub, and plasma TVs throughout the suite. There was even a plasma TV inside of the bathroom so you could relax in Jacuzzi tub.

Before I called Bryant, I got into the shower. I was starving. Bryant paid for this trip for me so I was going to take advantage of everything that made me happy. After the shower, I dried off and lotioned my body before I called Bryant. I kind of wanted him to think about me. I put one of my tight-fitting dresses on, my makeup, and locked my suite up. The restaurant was right on the resort. I walked and sat at the table to order my food. The waiter came and asked if I wanted some wine. I shook my head no and proceeded to look at the menu.

I order the steamed vegetables and grilled chicken with creamy chicken sauce and a dinner roll on the side. While my food was being prepared, I ordered my usual Remy VSOP on the rocks and I sat at the bar, watching my table. I grabbed my glass of Remy, walked back to my table, and waited for at least 10 minutes before my food arrived. The waiter walked up and put my plate of food on the table. You could smell the aroma from the food and it smelled so good that I couldn't wait to dig in, so I did.

I ate my food in peace. Jamaica was so laid back. It was palace that you could relax and get peace of mind.

Bryant drove up to the house. It was going on 8:00 P.M. After the barber shop, he went to the mall and bought some black and white Nike Airs. He walked to the front door, opened it, and walked upstairs to get ready to meet Mike. He turned he shower water on, laid his fresh, grey Nike sweat suit on the bed, and opened his drawer to get a fresh pair of white socks and boxers.

He looked at his cell phone and noticed Jocelyn didn't call him, so he called her.

Ring Ring

No answer. It went straight to voice mail. He left a message. Then, he hung up his phone and walked toward the bathroom to hop in the shower. Mike was calling his phone but there was no answer, so he left a voicemail for him to pick him up. After 20 minutes, Bryant got out of the shower, wrapped his towel around his waist, and walked in the bedroom. He noticed his phone lit up. He looked at it the phone. It said, *Missed Call*. He thought it was Jocelyn so he listened to the voicemail and noticed it was Mike.

He called Mike and Mike answered the phone.

"What's up, B, you still coming right?" Mike said to him.

"Yes, I am getting dressed right now. I will be there to get you in 20 minutes," said Bryant.

"Cool," Mike replied. They both hung the phone up. Bryant lotioned his body, grabbed his tank top and boxers, put his socks and sweat suit on, grabbed his Rolex out of his drawer, and went in the bathroom to brush his hair and spray his Eddie Bauer cologne.

He grabbed his fresh Nike tennis shoes and Jocelyn's car keys, walked down the steps, and before he walked toward the door, he felt he was missing something. He checked his pockets and he didn't have his phone or wallet. He ran back upstairs in the room and grabbed his cell phone and wallet. He attempted to call Jocelyn again but her voicemail came back on. He refused to leave another message for Jocelyn. He put the alarm on, left out, and started the car.

The wheels were shining and the car smelled so fresh. He had taken the car to the car wash earlier that day so he could surprise Jocelyn when she came home. He drove from the drive way and called Mike. Thirty minutes later, he arrived at Mike's beautiful mansion. Mike lived by himself in a four-bedroom, 2000-acre, two-level home. Bryant drove up his long driveway and parked in front of his house.

Bryant thought to himself, *Mike is getting this money for real.* Mike also owned a clothing business. He had two stores in New York and a shoe store in Atlanta, Georgia. As soon as Bryant walked up the walkway and rang the doorbell, Mike came to the door and opened it before he rang the doorbell again.

"What up, my nigga?" Mike said, smiling at Bryant.

"I see you are doing real big. How's the house coming along?" said Bryant.

"You know me, I can't complain. I been here for a couple of months, nothing major," said Mike. "You want something to drink before we leave?" Mike said.

"You know this, man," said Bryant.

They both walked toward the bar that was in the living room area.

"Man, this shit I see on TV," said Bryant.

Mike's crib was laid out. The living room was cherry wood, hardwood floor, five fireplaces throughout the house, customer kitchen with waterfall granite counters, and stone slab flooring. Mike showed Bryant the movie theater in the basement of his home with 12 German leather seats, equipped with Macintosh. They walked back upstairs and Mike showed Bryant the 70-foot infinity edge pool, heated spa, and flat backyard completely fenced.

"You know I'm your man. How much was this house, Mike?" Bryant asked.

"It was around 12 million, but I talked them down to 10 million. I paid straight cash," Mike said.

They gave each other a handshake while pouring some Remy and Alize from the bar. Bryant looked at his watch and noticed the time.

"Chill, man, hookers don't start coming out until 11:00 P.M.," said Mike. Mike walked through the kitchen to get to the spare room. He waved his hand so Bryant could follow him. Mike opened the room door and walked inside. Bryant walked inside the room and was so surprised. Mike had a big radio sound system, a 60-inch TV mounted on the wall, and a center stage with two swings and two stripper poles.

Mike said, "Welcome to the bunny lounge." He turned the disco light on to shine the room up.

"Man, you got it made," said Bryant.

Mike smiled and said, "I really don't come out. I have everything I need right here."

Bryant took another sip and gave Mike a handshake. They walked out of the room. Bryant asked Mike for the direction to the bathroom. Mike point to the direction, down the hall, and to the right. Bryant walked in the bathroom and noticed the big, long mirror vanity on the wall. Everything was trimmed in gold. The walk-in shower and the Jacuzzi bath tub were next to each other.

It even had his and hers toilets. He thought to himself; *why in the hell Mike need all this space?* He flushed the toilet, washed his hands, used the cocoa butter, and walked out of the bathroom. Mike was at the front door waiting.

Bryant walked outside and was getting ready to get in his car until Mike said, "Hey, come ride with me."

They walked toward the car garage. Mike wanted to drive his Rolls Royce. "Damn, nigga, you got three toys to choose from," Bryant said.

Mike smiled and said, "You ready? Which one?"

Mike walked toward the 2001 Lexus GS 300 and said, "We going to keep it simple tonight."

They both got in the car. Mike played his Juvenile CD and drove off. After driving 40 minutes in Atlanta, Mike drove in front of the Cheetah's Lounge and then grabbed his 45 pistol from under the driver's seat, put it in his pants, and stopped in front of the bell men to get his car parked.

Bryant got out of the car first and then Mike grabbed his cell phone and wallet. They both walked in. Mike was a regular there and had a VIP table all ready for him. That was Bryant's first time there, so Mike wanted to make it special for him. As soon as they walked toward their table upstairs, the waiter asked if there was anything they needed before the show started.

"Yes, get me some honey barbecue wings and a 5th of Remy and Alize blue, please," Mike said.

"Yes, get me some spicy honey barbecue wings with ranch dressing on the side," said Bryant. The waiter shook her head okay and then walked away, behind the bar.

The DJ spoke loudly on the mic, "now performing Miss Sunshine."

The waiter brought their food and bottles of Remy and Alize. "This must be somebody new," Mike said to Bryant. Sunshine came out onstage with a see-through sequined black dress and she wore a black bob and long knee-high boots. Bryant could not take his eyes off her. He fell in love with a fantasy.

Sunshine got on her knees and looked right at Mike and Bryant. She began taking all of her clothes off, wearing nothing but a black thong. Bryant stood up and watched her up and down.

Mike was hungry. He was eating his chicken that he ordered and then he poured them a cup of Remy and Alize mixed together. Sunshine was dancing so seductively until Bryant noticed who she was. They both made eye contact and Bryant shook his head. It was Saniyah. But, Saniyah didn't care, she was still performing. She looked at Bryant and bent over to touch her ankles. Bryant sat down and looked at Mike, but Mike was steadily eating his chicken and dancing to the music.

Bryant needed a drink fast. He drank his cup with one gulp. "Man, oh, man," he said to himself silently.

Sunshine kept performing for five minutes and then she left the stage. Dollars were everywhere, filling the stage. She switched her ass behind the curtains so the next dancer could perform.

"You enjoying yourself, my nigga?" Mike asked Bryant.

"You know me, I am chilling and observing," said Bryant.

"My bitch is getting ready to perform-Diamond," Mike said.

While Diamond was dancing and performing onstage, Mike got up and walked downstairs to get to the front of the stage. Bryant was alone until Saniyah walked upstairs and asked for a private dance. They both got up and walked in a closed off corner so that nobody could see them.

Bryant could not resist Saniyah after that time they had sex. He was hooked on her. He sat down in the lounge chair and reached in his pocket for money. He took out a stack of money and counted five 20 dollar bills. Saniyah laid him back and got on top of him like she was riding his cock.

Bryant was turned on. She began unbuttoning his pants and took out his hard-rock cock. She got up from on top of him and began dancing seductively; shaking her ass and making it jiggle in front of him while he was stroking his cock up and down. She grabbed both of her breasts and grabbed his cock between them. She got on her knees and then began kissing the top part of his cock, stroking back and forth and then began to suck on it, tightening her jaws and moving her head up and down slowly.

Bryant moaned silently. He grabbed the back of her head to go faster and faster, devouring all of his juices. Saniyah took one of his fingers and began sucking his it. She climbed on top of him, inserted his cock into her creamy canal, and began riding him slowly. Bryant was so horny. Jocelyn was gone for days and he needed sex so badly.

Saniyah moaned and moaned. He grabbed the back of her ass so she could ride him staying in one position. Saniyah kissed his lips and they began tongue kissing. They looked into each other's eyes, desiring for more and more. He flipped her over and began pounding her deeper and deeper from behind, holding both of her arms behind her back.

"Hey, Daddy, long time, no sees," Diamond said to Mike.

Diamond was his main bitch. He paid her $300 every time he saw her. "You coming home with me tonight?" he asked her.

"You know I am, Daddy," she said, as she was giving him a lap dance in the corner area.

"Damn, you going to make a nigga cum in his pants," said Mike.

"You here by yourself?" she whispered in his ear.

"No, my man somewhere with one of them hoe," said Mike.

"You ready to go or something?" Mike asked.

"Yes," she whispered in his ear.

Mike couldn't wait. Diamond walked from out of the corner and walked behind the stage to get dressed. He text Bryant's phone that he was leaving because he had business to take care of. Bryant looked at his phone. He received the message as Saniyah was putting on her clothes and she grabbing her money on the table. She gave Bryant a kiss on his lips and walked out of the corner. She hurried up behind the curtain so Mike wouldn't recognize who she was.

Bryant fixed his clothes, grabbed his cell phone and walked out five minutes after her. He walked toward

Mike and said, “Wait for me. I am going to the bathroom.”

“I got you,” said Mike. Bryant walked toward the men’s bathroom, washed his hands, and left out quickly.

They walked out of the club together and Diamond was waiting for her man. The bell man drove his car in front of him. He reached down in his pocket and gave him a 20 dollar tip. They both got into the car and Diamond got in the backseat.

“B, that’s Diamond,” said Mike.

Bryant turned his head around to her and said hello.

“You straight? We drunk the shit out of them bottles,” said Mike.

“Yes, I enjoyed myself,” said Bryant, smiling at the same time. They finally drove up to Mike’s driveway.

Bryant got out of the car, walked toward his car, got in, and waved goodbye to Mike and Diamond. He drove off quickly. He couldn’t wait to get home. It was 3:28 a.m. He knew he had to pick Jocelyn up from the airport the next evening.

His cell phone rang and it was Saniyah. “Hello,” said Bryant.

“Did you enjoy me?” said Saniyah.

Bryant laughed. “You funny, Sunshine. That’s your name, huh?” Bryant asked.

“Yes, that’s me,” said Saniyah.

“How long have you been doing this and what about the shop?” Bryant asked.

“I still have the shop. I just do this part-time,” said Saniyah.

"Well, I am tired. I have to talk to you some other time and try not to call me a lot, Jocelyn will notice," Bryant said.

"Oh, so you and Jocelyn still hanging on ya'll marriage?" Saniyah asked.

"Of course. Until death does us apart," Bryant said and then he hung the phone up before Saniyah replied.

Bryant drove into his driveway, turning his cell phone off. *Boy, oh, boy, I am tired*, he said to himself. He walked to the front entrance of his walkway and noticed a black car with tinted windows parked on the side of his house.

When he put the keys inside the lock, a man with a deep voice said, "Give it up, nigga."

Bryant tried to turn his head around to notice the man's face, but he heard a click from the gun. The man fired off the gun twice and Bryant fell to the ground.

The man reached inside of Bryant's pocket, grabbed a knot full of money, and left the scene quickly, running down the street. The car sped off, driving in the direction of the man. Bryant was holding his side. He knew it may have been a setup. Somebody was watching him and Saniyah from the strip club and followed him to Mike's house then to his house. Bryant reached in his pocket to grab his cell phone to call the ambulance.

Twenty minutes later, the ambulance came to take him to the nearest hospital. He was shot twice, once in his upper back and on the side of his stomach. Bryant was in so much pain. The detectives were eager to question him, but the nurses told them they had to call back. The nurse asked Bryant for an emergency contact but he couldn't respond. He had to go in surgery quickly to get the bullet out of his upper back.

A couple of hours later, Bryant were in recovery, but sore. The nurse kept checking on him and checking all of his vitals. He didn't want to call anybody and get them alarmed, so he rested until it was time for him to come get me from the airport the next day.

The detective came to his room and asked him a couple of questions. Bryant told them that somebody followed him home, robbed him, and that he wanted a patrol car in front of his house for a couple of weeks until they were able to find who robbed him. Bryant gave them a description of the black car with tinted windows.

He stated to him that he was in fear for his twin girls and wife. The detective did a full report and got all of Bryant's information and all contacts. The nurse stated to Bryant that he was able to go home the next day. Bryant called ADT to get a sensor installed for the front porch, back porch, garage, and front entrance so the lights were able to come on once the cars or a person was at the front or back door. Bryant was released at 7:15 a.m. He rushed home in pain to make sure the house was clean and there was no blood at the front of the door. There was a puddle of blood, so he got some bleach and hot water to soak the spot. It was still there so he drove to Home Depot, which was ten minutes away, and bought another door rug for the porch so the spot was not noticeable.

He had to meet the ADT system installer in 30 minutes at the house, so he drove quickly, going over the speed limit. He arrived at the driveway and the ADT van was parked in front of the house. He looked at the watch and asked the installer how many hours it would take to install.

"I just need one hour," the installer replied.

"Cool. I'm going to hop in the shower and go pick my wife up at 4:00p.m.," Bryant said to him.

Bryant put his cell phone on the charger and when he turned his cell phone back on, he had 20 messages. He knew that half of them were my messages. He hurried up, took his clothes off, walked in the bathroom, and turned the shower water on.

Something Feels Strange
Chapter 12

"Okay, Jamaica, time to go. I miss home," I said to myself, looking at the room and packing my suitcase. The plane landed at the airport in Atlanta. I missed Bryant. It felt like I hadn't seen my husband in a month. Bryant was standing there waiting on me. He smiled.

"I miss you," he said to me, giving me a big kiss on the lips.

I gave him a strange look and smiled. "I miss you, too, babe."

He opened my door, took my suitcases, and put them in the trunk. "Babe, has mom called you to check on the girls?" I asked him.

"Nope, babe, I called and left a message," said Bryant.

"I'm sure they are okay," he replied.

"I'm exhausted and hungry," I said to him.

"Look, babe, we can go out to dinner. Why don't you relax for a couple of hours while I go and check on something for Mike," he said.

"That's what I was planning on doing, babe, I'm tired," I said to him.

We arrived at the house and Bryant's phone rang. "Hello," said Bryant.

"Hey, sir, I left the instructions on the table. Call ADT if you have any questions," the installer said.

"Will do, and thanks," Bryant said, hanging the phone up so I couldn't hear his conversation.

"Who was that, Bryant?" I asked.

"Telemarketer, babe, trying to sell something, that's all," Bryant said to me.

Home sweet home, I said to myself when we arrived. I noticed a pretty, grassy looking rug on the porch. I asked Bryant about it and he stated that he wanted to surprise me and make the porch look more elegant for the family. I smiled and gave him a kiss on the cheek.

Bryant was so sweet. He walked me upstairs to the bedroom, laid me down on the bed, took my sandals off, and told me to wait and don't say a word. He ran downstairs to the car, watching his surroundings and took the suitcases out of the trunk to put them in the house. Before he attempted to close the door, he noticed a police car outside of the house and knew I was going to question him.

His shoulder was beginning to hurt because he was lifting heavy stuff and he knew the doctors told him that he could not do anything physical or athletic for a while. He left the suitcase by the door and walked to the kitchen to grab a bottle of water so he could take his pain medicine.

"Babe, is everything alright?" I yelled downstairs to him.

"Babe, chill, I'm okay," Bryant yelled in pain.

Knock Knock Knock

Then the doorbell rang from the front door.

I tip-toed out of the bed to look through the blinds to see who it was. It was two police officers. *What in the hell my husband got himself into?* I thought to myself. Bryant was the quiet type. I would never believe that he could hurt anybody.

"Hello, sir, sorry to disturb you," said the police officer.

"No worry," said Bryant. Bryant closed the door and gave the officer the look and pointed upstairs that I was resting.

"No problem, sir, just wanted to let you know that we are parked out here for the rest of the night," said the police officer.

"Thanks, I appreciate this. I have not told the wife what happened yet, didn't want to alarm her, you know how women are," Bryant said to the officer.

"Gotcha, we right out here if you need us, sir," said the officer, as he walked down the steps to get in the patrol car. Bryant closed the door gently.

When he turned around, I was right there. "Damn, baby, you scared the hell out of me," Bryant said.

"What is going on, Bryant?" I asked him, with my arms crossed, looking very angry.

"Babe, stop, nothing, we had a burglary across the street and they are just alarming everybody and watching for any activities, that's all," Bryant said, hugging me and grinding on me.

I couldn't resist him those dimples and that chocolate always had me week in the knee. We both walked upstairs. I got in the bed and Bryant took my clothes off, massaged my feet with oil, and we made passionate love. He kept his T-shirt on for some reason. Maybe he was cold. I didn't question him. I closed my eyes and went to sleep.

Bryant got up, walked into the bathroom, washed up and walked in the bedroom to put on another white T-shirt and a pair of his Armani jeans and brown butternut Timberland boots that he never wore. He kissed me on my forehead, grab his truck keys, and left out of the house, putting the alarm on. He opened the car garage up, parked my car inside of the garage, and drove his truck from out of the garage, and then drove off.

His phone rang. "What's up, nigga," Mike said.

"Man, I don't conversate over the phone, but I got to holla at you about something very important," said Bryant.

"Cool, meet me at the spot," said Mike.

"On my way," Bryant said.

After driving 40 minutes from the house, he finally arrived at Mike's house. Mike was waiting outside of the front door, waiting for him to arrive. Bryant jumped out of the truck and gave Mike some dap. "Man, oh, man," said Bryant.

"What's up," said Mike. They both walked inside of Mike's house and walked toward the living room, sitting on the couch.

Bryant walked toward the bar to pour him a glass of Remy and ice. Mike walked into the kitchen to grab his Gin and juice from out of the refrigerator. "Nigga, I got robbed," Bryant said to Mike, giving him a strange look.

"What?" said Mike.

"I got shot twice in my shoulder and the side of my waist," said Bryant.

"Hell, no, nigga. What's good? Who did that shit?" Mike screamed.

"I don't know. This shit happened in front of my fucking door," said Bryant.

"Fuck no, nigga, you don't have a strap?" Mike said, to him giving him eye contact.

"No, that's why I'm here. I got setup. Whoever did it followed me home from the strip club," Bryant said to Mike.

"You sure? That hoe didn't have anything to do with that?" said Mike.

"No, I know her, she knows better," said Bryant.

"Nigga, you came here first. You sure they didn't follow you here?" said Mike.

"I don't know, man," said Bryant.

Mike paced around the house. He ran upstairs to his safe, opened it, and grabbed two of his guns. He walked downstairs and handed one of the guns to Bryant.

"My nigga, that's what I'm talking about," Bryant said.

"You get caught and snitch, I'm going to have to kill you," Mike said, smiling at Bryant.

"Nigga, fuck you," said Bryant.

They both walked over to the couch and started sipping their drinks. Then, they started talking about high school days and women. "Man, I remember when Jocelyn wouldn't give you the time of day," said Mike. "Now, she's your wife."

"Yes, man, she doesn't know what happened. If I tell her, it would only make it worse," Bryant said.

"No, keep that shit between you and me, man," said Mike.

"But, no, on the real, slim, we going to have to get them. Whoever done that shit be at that strip club," said Mike.

"True, true," Bryant said, sipping his glass of Remy. "Man, I better let that shit slid for right now, a nigga is getting ready to own the restaurant and shit. I can't do this right now," said Bryant.

"I feel you," said Mike.

"Let me go meet the owner at the spot and I'm going to holler at you later," said Bryant.

He got up from the couch, gave Mike a dap and hug, and left out. Just before he walked to the door, his phone vibrated and it was Jocelyn.

"Babe, I need you here with me," I said to him.

"Babe, I just left Mike. I got a surprise for you, so stay put," he says to me.

I was worried about Bryant, but didn't want him to get upset with me. I decided to go pour a glass of wine and call Saniyah. Her phone rang three times and then went to voicemail. I wanted to see her and see how the shop was coming along. I put on my jeans and buttoned up pink Baby Phat shirt and white princess Reebok tennis shoes.

I was looking so good. My personal trainer had everything on me toned. The Jamaican men couldn't resist me and called me their chocolate beauty queen. I loved the attention. If only my own husband gave me that attention, I wouldn't have to travel alone.

Ten minutes, later my phone didn't ring so I decided to go to the shop and get my hair done. The water from Jamaica had me looking a hot mess. Thanks to Bryant, my car was gassed up and smelling good. The patrol car was sitting outside of our house. It felt like I was the president's wife. I had never had an experience like that in our neighborhood. Bryant told me not to ask them questions, so I didn't.

The officer waved goodbye as I was driving out of my driveway. My phone rang and it was Saniyah.

"Hey, girl," I said to her, excited to hear her voice.

"Hey, lady," Saniyah said, sounding tired and low.

"What's up? I am on my way to the shop. Why don't you meet me there?" I asked her.

"Sure, babe, what time? Let me get dressed," said Saniyah.

"Thirty minutes away," I said to her.

After driving through the city of Atlanta, I really couldn't believe that we had a break-in on our street. We were suburban people and things like that just don't happen because the drama was mostly in the city. The shop was looking so plain. I knew I didn't own it anymore, but I still had some say-so to things, and I just got tired of the business. Bryant wanted me home with the girls. He told me to sell the shop for a good amount and I did. My home girl, Saniyah, wrote a check for $212,000 and bought the salon from me without any problem.

Saniyah was the best multimillion dollar real estate agent in Atlanta and California. She didn't have to work for anything. But she was just like me, always needed to do something and live in a wealthy area.

"Hey, girl," Shantrice said, once she saw me. "You look good. We miss you."

I smiled as I was getting out of my car and walking in the hair salon. Saniyah had changed the name to "Women with Class" hair salon. I loved it.

"Where's Saniyah?" Shantrice asked.

"She is on her way," I said to Shantrice.

"Your body is tasty, girl," Shantrice said, smiling.

She had everybody in the salon looking at my ass and chest. It had me blushing, but embarrassed, too. *Shit, I know I'm the shit. I worked hard having this body*, I thought to myself. Saniyah drove up on her motorcycle.

"That's the diva coming," Shantrice said.

I looked while she was walking in the door. Saniyah looked so good that if I was gay, I would have probably tried to sleep with her as soon as I saw her.

She was bad. She had on her leather leggings and leather vest with a black, short-sleeve that made her breasts lift up. Her hair was always fierce. She was mouthwatering.

"What's up, babe," Saniyah said, smiling at me.

"I'm ready," I said to her.

We hugged each other and then I walked over to her chair. It felt funny to be in a chair of what I owned, but it was cool.

"Give me that long, sexy, porn look," I said to Saniyah.

She smiled and said, "Yes, you are going to look sexy for Bryant."

"I always do, but this time I want to try something different and long," I said to her.

"I'm going to try black, 14-inch tracks on you," said Saniyah.

"Yes, that's fine with me, sis," I said to her.

Saniyah already had some good quality, track hair-Yaki silk that was very pretty. Once she took the hair out of the pack, everybody came over to feel the softness of it. In Atlanta, women were known to wear the short haircuts with color.

Bryant's Dream Came True

Chapter 13

"Good evening, sir," Bryant said to Mr. Rick Nelson.

"Hey, Mr. Bryant James Carter, what a pleasure to meet you," said Mr. Nelson.

"I am ready to take over," said Bryant. "I have five of the top chefs that worked in the restaurant who I worked with over the past four years and I have not had any complaints from anybody."

"I know, that's what I hear, too, so you can take over the restaurant and I know you are responsible, Bryant," Mr. Nelson said.

"I have a lot of paperwork to discuss with you. Did you want to take them home and discuss it with your wife?" Mr. Nelson asked. Bryant giving him eye to eye contact.

"Yes, sir, I do, if it's okay. I would like for my lawyer to review it first for a day, then I will have these back to you with a check by the end of the week, if that's alright with you, sir," Bryant asked him.

"Sure, please take your time. I'm glad you are a responsible young man, Bryant. I owned Saskatoon Restaurant for 10 years now and it's time to retire. Business has been looking good. I'm getting older, I'm 68 years old," said Ricky Nelson.

"It's all good, sir, I will take care of the restaurant like I have been for four years," said Bryant.

They got up from the chair, shook each other's hand, and walked out of the café together. Bryant was so excited to tell me the great news. He called his attorney and she picked up quickly.

"I want to drop off some paperwork to you. Are you available now?" he asked.

"Yes, I'm in the office," she replied back to him.

It was a Saturday and his attorney was in the office, working like always. She never gets a vacation and was like a mom to Bryant. He got into his truck and drove off to meet her at her office 20 minutes away from the café where he met Mr. Nelson.

When he arrived, he walked into the building and spoke to the security officer that was on duty, and then walked upstairs to the 3rd floor, Suite 390l. As soon as she saw him, she gave him a big hug and kiss on his cheek.

"Hi, sweetie," Lauren smiled at him.

"I have something for you," he said to her. He handed her the paperwork and gave her a hug and kiss.

"Great! How you been and how's the family?" Lauren asked him.

"Everybody is doing great. The girls are getting big," he replied.

"How's Jocelyn Carter?" Lauren asked him.

"Can't complain. She is looking great and spending all our money," he said laughing and giggling.

"Well, as long as she happy, right?" Lauren said to him.

"Exactly," Bryant relied.

"I have to go home for dinner. I know you will take care of that for me; I will pick them up on Monday," he said to her.

"That's fine. You know tomorrow is church day for me," Lauren said. "You and Mrs. Carter should come to my church and visit Sunday," Lauren said.

"I can't promise you tomorrow, but one day, we will. If not Sunday, maybe bible studies," Bryant said to her, as he was walking out of the office.

"All done, Miss Lady," Saniyah said to me, with a smile.

I looked in the mirror. My hair was beautiful. I knew Bryant was going to love this hairstyle although I looked like Saniyah's twin. But, my hair was chic, bold, black, and beautiful. I jumped from the chair and attempted to pay Saniyah, but she refused. I gave her a big hug and waved goodbye to everybody at the shop, and then walked over to Shantrice and gave her a big hug. I walked toward the door, got in my car, and drove off before Bryant got home. I wanted to surprise him with champagne and candles throughout the house. After driving 20 minutes, going 70 mph, I drove up to my driveway and the unmarked police car was still there.

I walked to my front door and the light came on automatically. I put the keys in the door and walked in to put the alarm code on. *Bryant is going to love my hair,* I said to myself. I ran upstairs to run my bath water, opened the hallway closet door where I have all of my scented candles, grabbed 10 of them, lit all of them with my torch lighter, and put them throughout the house. I put three on the stairs, two on the end tables of the living room, one on the entertainment stand next to the TV, another one on the dining room table.

The other five I took upstairs and put them on our dresser and night stands, and turned Prince's *"Do Me Baby"* on repeat. I then hurried up to get in the warm bubble bath water before Bryant came home. Twenty minutes passed and I heard a loud voice from downstairs. I sprayed my perfume on, put on a satin, white a pair of my Victoria Secret sandals, and laid on the bed, waiting for Bryant to walk through the door.

I yelled, "I'm upstairs, babe."

"Babe, why do you have candles lit?" said Bryant, as he walked in the door.

His eyes got so big because he could not believe I had long hair. He smiled and walked toward me, noticing the scent of the candles and the sweet scent on my caramel body. He picked me up and said, "Baby, I'm going to eat you so good tonight."

"Baby, you like my hair?" I asked him.

"Like it? Baby, I love it," he said.

“Damn, I’m so hard for you,” he said, smiling and kissing my neck.

I love that man. All I could think about was him marrying me all over again. I never thought that he would hurt me ever again. Bryant laid me down so gently and stated that he wanted to make some something real special. The sound of Prince’s voice had me wanting him more and more. The desire I had for him was the same desire when we made love for the very first time.

Bryant kissed me gently and then walked downstairs to the kitchen. He wanted to cook me a chicken casserole. He was so excited to be the owner of the restaurant and he wanted me to try his first secret dish. Thirty minutes went by and Bryant poured me some White Zinfandel and prepared to dinner for us.

He walked upstairs with two plates, a bottle of champagne, and two wine glasses. “Baby, you are such a good husband. Let me help you, I insist,” I said to him.

“Baby, I got this. You just sit your pretty ass down and keep looking sexy for me. I’m going to feed you tonight and you are going to be my dessert,” Bryant said.

He switched the CD to Teena Marie’s “*Out on a Limb*.” Bryant was feeling some kind of way. As he was feeding me, the tears came down his face. Whatever my husband was going through, he didn’t want to tell me anything, but I would have found out.

Bryant poured us both a glass of champagne. We made a toast and promised to me that he was going to be the perfect man and that he loved me so much. ‘Til death do us part." I kissed my husband so gently on his lips, wiping the sweat from over his forehead.

I wanted some more of the casserole because it was so good. The broccoli and potatoes he added gave it a taste that was remarkable. “Baby, I’m going to hop in the shower. Give me 10 minutes and I’ll be right back,” said Bryant.

“Baby, I’m not going anywhere. I gave him eye contact, touched his sweaty face, and told him that I loved him and that I would die for him. Bryant looked at me for about five minutes with all types of thoughts running through his mind. He looked like he wanted to say something to me, but he didn’t.

He said, “I love you, too, baby,” kissed my forehead, and then walked toward the door, heading toward the bathroom. “Why, oh, why,” Bryant said to himself, looking at the mirror. “I can’t keep lying to my wife about her girlfriend and if tell her she is going to leave me,” he whispered, huffing and puffing. He ran the shower water, took off his shirt, and got into the shower. He reached to hold the side of his stomach which was still sore and sat in the tub while the water covered his face. The Jacuzzi deep tub felt relief to him and he just laid there until he knew Jocelyn was asleep.

Grand Opening
Chapter 14

T

The ribbon was cut and the restaurant was now open for business. It was 9:05P.M. and the line was around the corner, waiting for the doors to open to Bryant's restaurant called, "Taste of Pleasures," previously named Saskatoon. I was so excited for him. Saniyah, Mike, and I were waiting for his grand entrance when the limo arrived. I stepped out looking like a don diva and Bryant was dressed in his satin, Versace suit. I had on my satin, silver Bebe knee-length dress. Saniyah's eyes got so big and Mike was smiling, but she looked puzzled. Bryant held my hand and we both walked toward the front door.

We felt like celebrities. Bryant was banking a grip every week and the restaurant was known for his favorite casserole that nobody prepared but him. He took the initiative to only work on Wednesdays which was free drink night.

That was the talk of the town. Women would ask Bryant if he would have sex with them. They were so upset with him that it was pathetic!

"Hey, girl, you look beautiful," Saniyah said. She had on her black Bebe dress which showed all of her curves, but my dress was the best. Bryant whispered in my ear how beautiful I looked!

"What up, my nigga?" said Mike, giving Bryant a hand shake and hug. "I told you, you getting this money," Mike said, smiling at Bryant.

The cameraman took a picture of him and Mike standing, holding each other's hand and smiling at each other. I was over there talking to one of the waitresses by the front door, saying, "Look at him. He is so happy."

She says, "Yes, he is, but it seems to me the young lady that's standing next to them is not so happy." Then she walked away. I gave her a bitch look and said to myself, *this hooker needs to be fired she must don't know who I am.* I attempted to approach her, but Saniyah walked up and gave me a hug. We all walked inside the restaurant.

Bryant looked puzzled, walking behind me. Saniya hand Mike walked behind him and all four of us walked toward the VIP section. I sat down with Mike and Bryant got up from the table.

"I'm coming back, babe, let me check on something," he said to me, and then walked toward the bar then around the corner.

"I'm going to powder my nose," Saniyah said, walking the same direction of Bryant. But, turned the corner walking toward the restroom. Bryant noticed and walked her direction so Jocelyn and Mike didn't notice them.

He grabbed Saniyah's arm and said, "come here, we need to talk," he said aggressively.

"Talk about what, Bryant?"

"Bitch, if you show any signs tonight about us and what happened, I swear I'm going to," Bryant said to her, giving her a mean look.

"Bryant, please, I'm so over your ass. You are not worth telling on," Saniyah said.

"That was a mistake, Saniyah, that shouldn't have happened," Bryant said.

"You right, a fucking mistake, now let's enjoy tonight," Saniyah said, walking away and switching her ass toward the bathroom. Bryant watched her seductively. He couldn't resist Saniyah; she had him hypnotized every time he saw her.

Bryant walked away toward the bar. While talking to Mike, I was not listening to anything he was saying, my mind was on Bryant. As he walked toward us with two bottles of Dom Perignon and four glasses, Saniyah walked behind him, "where's the drinks?" she replied. "I'm ready to party."

"Me, too," I yelled.

Bryant yelled out loud, "aye, you, D Man, crank that shit."

The DJ played music. Bryant grabbed my hand, poured four glasses of wine, and made a toast to life. We all put our glasses together and sipped our champagne. Bryant took me on the dance floor and we danced to his favorite music. Mike grabbed Saniyah's hand and she danced on him seductively, almost having Mike grab her ass. The dance floor was packed! The DJ had to slow it up, playing R. Kelly's "Slow Dance".

Bryant grabbed my ass so gently and caressed my back, kissing my neck. Saniyah looked at us both, giving us a look like she wanted to join in. Mike was now dancing with two light-skinned, pretty model women! Saniyah walked back to the table, poured her another glass of champagne, and sat down by herself. Bryant whispered in my ear how much he loved me and that he would never do anything to harm me.

I looked at him and said, "I know." We both danced the night away.

Ricky Nelson walked in and smiled at Bryant. "Hey, baby, I want you to meet somebody," he said, as we both walked toward Mr. Nelson.

"Bryant, my man, congratulations," said Mr. Nelson.

Bryant shook his hand, smiled and said, "Mr. Nelson, this is my lovely wife, Mrs. Jocelyn Carter."

"Hello, madam," said Mr. Nelson, as he kissed on hand.

"It's a pleasure to finally meet you, Mr. Nelson. I heard a lot about you," I said to him, giving him straight eye contact. "Baby, I'm going to check on Saniyah. I'll be right back."

Bryant and Mr. Nelson walked by the DJ upstairs to Bryant's personal office.

"Hey, girl," I said to Saniyah, surprising her.

"So, Jocelyn, how things been going with you and Bryant?"Saniyah asked.

I knew what Saniyah was up to. She's always been jealous of me and Bryant and she was going to tell me how she was so happy for us and that I should always keep my eyes open. "Girl, Bryant is going to be Bryant. I love that man," I said to her.

"Yes, Bryant going to be Bryant," she said, with a smirk on her face, smiling and sipping her champagne. "I'm going home Jocelyn. I think I had too much to drink," said Saniyah.

"You want me to drive you home, sis?" I asked her.

"No, Mike is going to take me home. He picked me up," said Saniyah.

Mike walked up and said, "Your drunk ass ready?"

"Yes," Saniyah said, giving him a drunken look.

"You'll make sure you all call me," I said to them both as they both walked toward the front entrance of the restaurant. I sat there for 30 minutes until Bryant finally walked downstairs with Mr. Nelson. Bryant shook his hand and Mr. Nelson walked toward the entrance to leave.

"Baby, you ready?" said Bryant.

"Ready as I'm ever going to be," I said to him.

"Saniyah, you are ridiculous," said Mike. "You need to stop drinking if you can't handle it," he yelled.

"Nigga, I'm a grown ass woman. Your man shouldn't be acting like we never had sex together," she blurted out her mouth.

"My man, who, Saniyah?" Mike said.

"Ha, don't act like he never told you we had sex, Mike," Saniyah said, turning her back toward him while he was talking to her. Saniyah went to sleep.

Mike was confused and angry. He wanted to punch Bryant's eyes out. As soon as he drove up to Saniyah's house, he reached down in her purse and grabbed her house keys, opened the passenger door, and picked her limber body up. He walked toward her front door, kicked it open, turned her lights on in the living room, and laid her on the couch. Then, he took her heels off. Saniyah was so drunk, she didn't feel anything. He gently tip-toed out of the front, locking her bottom lock, jumped in the car, and sped off.

He dialed the numbers quickly on his cell phone and Bryant's voicemail picked up. Mike wanted to leave a grimy message, but he didn't. He decided to wait until the next day. After driving 30 minutes, he missed his exit. He was driving 70 mph to get home. Once he arrived, he drove up his long drive way. He walked into the front door of his house, turned off the alarm, lay on the couch, closed his eyes, and fell asleep in 10 minutes.

He was tired but still thought about what Saniyah told him.

"Baby, something felt strange tonight with you and Saniyah," I said to him, giving him an enraged look.

"Baby, what the hell are you talking about?" he replied, giving me a mad look.

"I know my friend; she is very sneaky," I said to him, while taking my dress off.

"Maybe she's not your friend, Jocelyn, if you have those thoughts in your head," Bryant replied.

"I hope you wouldn't stoop that low," I said to him, leaving out of the room, going into the bathroom.

Bryant lay on the bed and closed his eyes. He was upset that Jocelyn approached him that way. He reached in his pocket to grab his cell phone and turned it off. Bryant hated to turn his phone off because of emergencies, but he didn't want any disturbance.

I walked into the room, wearing my satin night gown, and laid beside him, but turned my back toward him. He huffed and puffed until he got up, walked toward the front door, and walked downstairs. I thought he was going to leave. Bryant is the guilty type. He leaves out when he's upset and don't come back until the next day. At this point, I didn't care, I was fed up! I felt something was wrong, maybe I needed another vacation. This time, I was going to snoop around and fake like I was going back to Jamaica.

My mind was on Victoria as if she was telling me to look out for cheating clues. I needed to meet her again, maybe tomorrow. I will call or email her so I can get some advice! I closed my eyes, grabbed my pillow, and dozed off to sleep. Bryant took his shoes off and lay on the couch. For some reason, he couldn't sleep. He wanted to confess to Jocelyn, but didn't know if she would leave him forever. He was weak for beautiful women and Saniyah was his type. He wanted to meet Saniyah in a couple of days to talk to her.

He reached down in his suit pocket, grabbed his cell phone, turned it on, and stood up to take his clothes off and socks and began texting Jocelyn, saying how much he apologized for his tone of voice, saying how much he loved her and that he learned his lesson from almost losing her from the car accident. When he was done with Jocelyn, he text Saniyah and asked when they could meet. He waited and waited for a response from Jocelyn or Saniyah for 30 minutes and then he closed his eyes and went to sleep.

Chapter 15 The Truth Shall Set You Free

"V

"Victoria, thanks for meeting me here at the park. How beautiful is the weather is today?" I said to her.

"No problem, Jocelyn, what bring you here? It sounded urgent."

"Victoria, I'm tired. Something is not right. I rather be alone then in pain," I said to her.

"What do you mean, Jocelyn?"

"I'm going to act like I'm going out of town to see what Bryant has up his sleeve. I need your help," I said to Victoria.

"Sure, you know I'm here," she said to me, smiling very mischievously.

"Today, I'm telling Bryant that I booked my flight for Jamaica again for me and one of my clients. I'll call my girlfriend Saniyah to offer her to go with me. She's going to say no and then I'm going to let her know I'm going to Jamaica," I said.

"Jocelyn, who is Saniyah?" Victoria asked me, looking me straight in the eye as if she knew I didn't like Saniyah too much.

"The bitch, Victoria, the bitch," I said to her.

"Are you sure, Jocelyn?" she asked me.

"No, I'm not sure. That's why I'm going to find out who he is cheating on me with," I said to her, leaning my head down with tears coming down my face.

"Jocelyn, you have to leave him here. I'm going to give you two big bottles of sulfuric acid," said Victoria. Wiping my tears from my face, I was so confused about what Victoria wanted me to do. I grabbed both of the glass, big bottles and put them in my backpack.

Victoria said, “You know what to do,” then she grabbed my hand and said, “God bless you.” Then, she walked away. I was emotional and had to sit on the bench thinking for another hour. I thought about my girls and jail time if I did anything to Bryant. I didn’t care. I was fed-up and depressed. I took two Adapin pills and drank my bottle of water.

My cell phone rang and it was Saniyah. “Hey girl, what’s up?” she said to me, sounding so happy.

“I’m relaxing, out doing some jogging. What’s good, sis?” I said to her, sounding fake as hell.

“I’m going out tonight and wanted to know if you wanted to go clubbing with me,” Saniyah asked.

“No, babe, I’m going to Jamaica Friday and won’t be back until the following Friday. Why don’t you come with me?” I asked her. “Please, Saniyah, you need to get away from that shop you work at," I said to her.

“Girl. People don’t have money like you and Bryant.” She smacked her teeth. “You go by yourself?”

“No, I have an old friend of mine that will be coming with me,” I said to her.

“Cool, well let me get dressed. I have to meet somebody later,” Saniyah said to me.

“You be safe tonight, girl,” I said to her, and then hung the phone up. I got up from the bench, grabbed my heavy book bag, and walked toward my car. I was still mad at Bryant but we were going to make up later on.

I called his phone and it went to voice mail. I left a sexy message for him and drove up in front of Lenox Square Mall to spend some of his money. I wanted to buy a new wig and shades to give me a different disguise. As soon as I got to the mall, I went directly to the wig outlet. This time, I knew I had the right amount of money. Bryant's credit card was loaded and I wouldn't even put a dent in it!

A couple hours went by and I called Bryant's Mom to check on the girls. They were coming home the following week and I was excited.

"Muah," I said to Aniyah, who always kept me on the phone for hours.

I drove up in front of the house and proceeded to walk in the door. I knew Bryant was going to be late tonight. I was tired from all that shopping. I had five bags, including my heavy book bag filled with two bottles of acid. I immediately walked in the garage and put them on the side of the wooden book shelf on the floor so I could hide them from the girls! I walked into the house and ran upstairs to put the bags down, grabbed my suitcase, and began packing as if I was going to Jamaica. Thirty minutes went by and Bryant walked in the house and yelled my name. "I'm upstairs, babe," I screamed back at him, responding.

"What are you doing?" he asked me.

"Packing, remember?"

"Ooh, that's right. I see you are really going to Jamaica, huh?" He grabbed me and gave me a soft kiss on my lips!

"I can't wait, babe, I am all prepared and got my flight tickets." I grabbed my purse and showed him the old flight tickets from before. He never even paid attention to the date to make sure! I hurried up and put them in my purser and tucked my purse under the bed while he was taking his shirt off, preparing for a hot shower

"Want to join me?" he asked me.

"No, babe, you go 'head. I want to make sure everything is packed up so I don't forget anything!"

Bryant walked to the bathroom and shut the door. I grabbed my cell phone and text Victoria. I was going to be with her. She was going to take me to a secluded hotel one hour from where we lived and was going to be my look out girl.

Vicky, I'm supposed to be headed out tomorrow. Don't forget our plan. I didn't want to wait for her response but I knew she was going to be at the airport around 6:00 a.m. to meet me with an unmarked car! I put my phone on the charger and waited for Bryant to turn the water on so I could hide the items I packed in my bag. The water finally stopped. I hurried up and grabbed my heavy suitcase from off the bed, onto the floor, grabbed my robe, and hurried to take my clothes off by the time Bryant walked in the door.

I was already undressed. "Babe, I'm going to get in the shower and go straight to sleep to get on this flight tomorrow," I said.

"I know, babe," said Bryant.

I walked passed him into the bathroom. Bryant watched me as I walked in the bathroom and closed the door behind me.

Two Can Play These Games
Chapter 17

Beep Beep

"Come on, babe. You take forever. You know you can't miss your flight," Bryant yelled, while beeping the horn. I grabbed my purse and black bobbed wig with black sunglasses as I was walking toward the front door. Outside, I noticed Victoria was parked on the side of the house in an unmarked Grand Marquis, dark blue car.

"Sorry, babe, I almost forgot my makeup and you know I can't leave home without my mask," I said to Bryant.

"I don't know why you wear that shit, anyway," he said to me, giving me straight, eye contact. Bryant used to love me in makeup. Our marriage had not been the same lately. I wanted to catch him red-handed. As soon as he backed up from the car garage, Victoria waited for 15 minutes and drove right behind us! She knew I was going to the Jacksonville airport in ATL.

As soon as we arrived, Bryant put his hazard lights on and was eager to help with my luggage. He opened the trunk and walked my items to the inside of the airport. I looked at my side view and I noticed Victoria's car.

"Baby, you sure you don't want to come?" I asked him, smiling and giving him a kiss on his soft lips.

"No, baby, you enjoy this time alone," said Bryant. We hugged each other goodbye and tongue kissed for 10 minutes. The passion I had for my husband was always there, but the trust wasn't. I walked away from him, rolling my suit suitcases and purse on my shoulder. He watched me as I walked through the gates, then he left out of the airport. He would have never thought that I was hiding around that corner. I immediately went inside of the bathroom, reached down in my purse, and put on my black bobbed wig and black sunglasses. I also changed my clothes, wearing a big T-Shirt and sweat pants. When I walked out of the bathroom, Victoria came to the rescue. I watched her drive up, waiting for me to come outside. I knew Bryant drove off and wasn't going to look back.

I walked toward the car and she pushed the trunk button. I put both of my suitcases in the trunk, and then got in the passenger seat. Victoria looked at me and smiled. Our plan was to drop me off at the Enterprise rental car place across from the Holiday Inn an hour away from my house. Victoria was quiet. She was an expert on catching her husband cheating, so she didn't really say a word. I needed a drink so badly, so my first stop was going to be somebody's liquor store, buying me a 5th of Remy!

As soon as she arrived at the Enterprise, I got out of the car, opened her trunk, and grabbed both of my suitcases. Then, I walked inside of the Enterprise to get my rental car that I reserved a week ago. Everything was all planned out! I was very particular on what I wanted to drive. I had to be low-key so Bryant wouldn't notice who I was. A flashy car was not the plan. The lady handed me the keys to a black Nissan Sentra.

Victoria waited until I walked outside. She noticed me opening the door and dangling the keys. That was my signal for her to leave and wait for my text. Victoria beeped the horn and drove off, heading the opposite direction. I got into the Nissan Sentra and drove out from the garage, heading toward the hotel. I looked at my watch again. I was right on schedule, so I could finally rest until the next day. I drove in front of the Holiday Inn and parked the car in the underground garage. I took the elevator to the first floor where the concierge desk was.

"Reservations for Mrs. Carter," I stated to the older lady that was at the desk.

I handed her my American Express credit card. She looked in the system and handed me the key card to check in. My room was on the 4th floor. I needed that exercise, so I carried all of my luggage and purse and headed toward the door to get to my studio suite.

I was opening the door, trying to rush to get in. By now, I was out of fucking breath. I lugged those heavy ass bags down in front of the door and headed straight to the bed to take off my clothes and shoes to rest. I was trying to clear my bad thoughts about Saniyah and Bryant on how they were acting strange at Bryant's grand opening. That made me felt suspicious about their body language toward each other. I wanted to get to the bottom of things and I knew Victoria was going to help me!

Bryant was timing me from the time I left the Jackson Ville airport to the time I landed in Jamaica, so I knew I had to call him in one hour. I looked at my Chanel watch and I had time to take a 45-minute nap. I set the clock on my cell phone, and then dozed off to sleep.

Ring Ring

Ring Ring

One hour later, I got up quickly. It was Bryant. I looked at the phone and noticed I had 15 missed calls. I hurried up and ran into the bathroom, turned on the water, and washed my face. I walked in the kitchenette area and grabbed a bottle of water from out of the fridge and downed it like I was on somebody's desert.

I grabbed my cell phone and hurried up to call Bryant. Before I called him, I ran to turn the radio on as if I was having fun and not sounding depressed.

Ring Ring

He quickly answered the phone, "hello."

"Hey, baby, I didn't even hear the call. The phone was in my purse," I quickly said to him.

"I was worried, babe, you know how I get when you on them planes," Bryant replied.

"I know. I was waiting on the shuttle and it finally came and now I'm on the resort. They're having some type of festival down here," I said to him.

"Is that why I hear all that music in the background?" Bryant said.

"Yes, I'm having a great time. I wish you could have come, but I know you have the restaurant to look after," I said to him.

"You know I'm a hardworking man, babe. I'm about to take a shower and head to the restaurant," Bryant replied.

"Cool, good stuff, babe. I love you and I will make sure I will call you bright and early," I said to him.

We both gave each other a kiss good night then hung the phone up at the same time. "Woo!" I said, sitting on the bed. I was so eager to catch Bryant in the act. Victoria was supposed to be outside of the house, taking pictures and watching his every move for a couple of days until the Friday when I was going to arrive at the house. I forgot to put the Remy Martin bottle in the refrigerator. I walked to open the blinds, lit a cigarette that I really needed at the moment, and poured a glass of Remy straight, no chaser, and one cube of ice, took two big sips, and puffed my cigarette. I was so relaxed!

I grabbed my cell phone to call my mom. I knew she was up. I still had to lie to her about being in Jamaica.

Ring Ring Ring

"Hello," she answered in her seductive voice as usual.

"Hey, Mom, it's me," I said to her.

"Hey, baby girl, what's wrong?" she replied.

"I just have a lot on my mind and I needed your advice," I said to her.

"Where are you, Jocelyn?" she asked.

I hesitated for about 10 seconds, but answered her.

"I'm in Jamaica. Me and Bryant."

"Oowee, why you went back there?" she asked.

"Me and him needed some alone time away from the girls. He's downstairs at the bar. I'm getting ready to meet him once I get out of the shower."

"What's on your mind, baby?" Marilyn asked.

"Mom just wanted to tell you that I love you. That is all," I said to her, trying to hold back my tears.

"I love you, too, always know that God has a purpose for us," she said to me. My mom was very religious. She would always make me go to church every Sunday and bible studies on Tuesdays. After my dad passed away, she found herself more and more in church, seven days a week. She would hardly ever be home. I don't know how I caught her on this day of the week. Before I got off the phone with her, I let her know that Bryant and I would be separated soon.

She didn't question me for some reason. My mom knew all these years that Bryant and I were together that she felt Bryant was betraying me, but didn't want to let me know. All she said before I got off the phone with her was, "everything happens for a reason, baby girl, remember that."

I kissed her goodbye on the phone and then hung up. My mom showed no remorse. It was like she was giving me a good sign, or maybe that was the Remy talking to me. The rest of the night, I smoked cigarettes and poured two more glasses of Remy. After that, I went to sleep thinking about Bryant all night and wondering if he was thinking about me or another woman.

Deadly Decisions
Chapter 18

S

Saniyah came the next day around 4:00P.M.She parked her car in the driveway as soon. As she got out of the car, she looked around to see if anybody noticed her coming up the front steps.

Bryant opened the door and peeped outside. Once Victoria noticed Saniyah getting out of the car, she took five pictures with her digital camera, standing beside her unmarked car, which was parked on the side of the end house on the street.

"Hurry up and come inside," Bryant said, giving her full eye contact.

"What's wrong? Why you are so nervous?" Saniyah asked him.

"I'm not nervous. There are just some nosey ass neighbors we have around here and they may think you are another women creeping to see me," Bryant said to her.

"I am," Saniyah said as she walked toward him, grabbing the side of his face and kissing his lips gently.

Bryant grabbed her hand and said, "Wait, we need to talk."

They both walked toward the couch and then Bryant walked toward the bar, pouring them both two glasses of Hennessy on the rocks.

"You know what this leads up to, Bryant," Saniyah said to him, grabbing the glass from out of his hands.

"I know, that's why I called you over here so we can put a stop to this," he said to her, turning his back toward her and walking toward the couch.

"Saniyah, I can't fucking do this no more. Something is going to have to give, fuck," he yelled, with his head turned down.

"Look at me, Bryant, we both love what we do. Jocelyn is never going to find out and, if she does, I will never tell," said Saniyah.

"I know. I just don't want my marriage to end, but I can't stop thinking about you."

He took a big sip of his glass and laid it on the end table. "Bryant, I'm sorry what I said to you at your grand opening. I was just upset," she said.

She walked toward him, holding her glass. She took a big sip, put it on the wooden bar, and then walked toward him and grabbed his waist, kissing him on the back of neck. Bryant grabbed her hands tightly enjoying every urge that he had for her. They both walked upstairs toward the bedroom! Saniyah laid him on the bed and began taking her clothes, off leaving only her red bra and red lace panties on.

Bryant watches her caramel-brown body, picturing her dancing on the pole. He took his sweat pants off, only wearing his boxers and tank top. Saniyah walked toward him with her seductive walk and reached down to grab his cock and devour him inside her warm mouth. Bryant moaned and moaned, grabbing the back of her neck, and then rubbing her hard nipples inside her bra. They began making love for an hour, falling asleep for a couple of hours. When Bryant woke up, Saniyah was gone, leaving a note saying that she will call him tomorrow, she had to perform tonight.

Bryant looked at the clock. It was 10:00P.M. He hurried up and got up and ran down the stairs to find his cell phone. He looked on the couch and then looked on the bar. His phone was nowhere to be found. He then looked in the kitchen and there it was, on the breakfast counter on vibrate. He noticed Jocelyn didn't call and that seemed so strange, so he called her.

Ring Ring Ring

Her phone went to voicemail and he left her a message. He waited for her to call back for hours. He walked upstairs to clean the bedroom, trying to clean up all evidence and smell. He grabbed the sheets and comforter from off the bed, walked downstairs to the laundry room, and put them in the washing machine.

"Victoria, you sure that was Saniyah or Cindy?" I asked her, sounding so depressed. I shared more tears than I expected and my heart was beating fast.

"Jocelyn, she's tall, caramel-complected, petite, long hair, and drives a red Infiniti.

"Yes, that's Saniyah," I said to Victoria.

"Well, like you said, your instinct doesn't tell a lie. I took pictures and uploaded them to your email address so you can see for yourself," Victoria said to me.

"I believe you, Victoria, that's why you are my friend. From the first day you purchased those items for us, I knew you kept it real," I said to her.

"Jocelyn, be strong. I'm heading home. Your husband has not left the house all day, so sleep on it until Friday when you catch his ass red-handed. I guarantee you she will be back to see him," Victoria said before she hung up the phone.

I hung up, too, and got up from the bed. I looked around and it was a mess in that hotel room. I was so depressed and have been crying and moping around all day. Not only was my husband cheating on me, but he cheating on me with my best friend/my kids' god mother, and they're fucking in my house. I wanted to call him so badly, but didn't know if I could take any more of his lies.

I walked into the bathroom and turned on the shower water, steaming the mirrors up. I stood in front of the mirror, wiping in a circular motion, looking at myself in the mirror. I had not eaten in a couple of days and I knew if I left that hotel room, I wasn't going to come back.

So, I looked in the mirror and really couldn't understand why my husband and best friend betrayed me. *Who would have thought?* I said to myself, as the tears ran down my face, feeling like I needed to be in Saint Elizabeth. I thought I was going crazy and I felt nauseous. I opened the toilet and began to vomit, and then cry, and then vomit, holding my head and my stomach, thinking to myself, *this man is going to put me in the hospital*. "Why, God, oh, why?" I yelled, crying and crying. I finally got the strength to get up from the floor and took off my clothes, looking at my fragile little body in the mirror, noticing the 15 pounds I had lost in two weeks.

I stepped in the shower and lay there on my back, legs straight, like I was already dead. After reviewing the picture for an hour through my email, I decided to call Bryant. I had a long talk with him and he made it even worse by lying to me, but I kept it cool like Victoria told me to do. I followed all of her directions. I couldn't wait until tomorrow night; that was the only thing on my mind.

"Okay, baby, I love you. Can't wait to see you Sunday," I said to him, giving him a big kiss over the phone.

I closed my laptop and put my cell phone on the charger. I wanted to grab something to eat and head to the liquor store before it closed. So, I hurried up to put a pair of baggy jeans on, a hoodie, and a pair of New Balance tennis shoes. I grabbed the car keys and key card and left out of the hotel room, wearing a Yankee fitted hat.

The front desk attendant thought I was a man. She said, “Have a good night, sir.” I kept walking!

I drove to the liquor store and up to the drive-through window. “A fifth of Remy VSOP, please, and a pack of Newport cigarettes.” I gave him my credit card he handed me the bag. Then, I drove off, desperately in need of a smoke. I opened the pack of Newport’s, lit a cigarette, and drove up to the McDonald’s drive-through 10 minutes away from the hotel.

“Excuse me; can I have a fish meal with a Sprite drink?” I yelled in the intercom. Once I drove around, I noticed I didn’t have my cell phone, so I hurried to grab my food, paid the lady, and drove to the hotel.

When I arrived, I hurried up to my room, got on the elevator, and hurried to eat my food. I was so hungry that it felt like I hadn’t eaten in months. That fish sandwich was so good my mouth was watering for it! As soon as I got in the room, I put my 5th of Remy VSOP bottle in the mini refrigerator and walked to grab my phone off the charger, hoping that Bryant left a message or voicemail. Instead, there was nothing. I deleted the one from earlier. Bryant was being Bryant, as usual. I ate the rest of my food, turned the TV on to watch some news, and then dozed off to sleep.

"You have a new message," my cell phone operator said. It was Victoria letting me know that Bryant left out of the house. It was 5:00A.M. in the morning. I knew Bryant was jogging around at this time and on his way to the gym. She also text me that there was the same red car that was parked the day before that just arrived before he left the house. I thought to myself, *what the hell Saniyah doing over there that time of morning?* Saniyah only wanted Bryant for his money. She was the gold-digging type and would fuck anybody who offered her money. A scandalous, smart whore that knew what the hell she was doing.

I closed my eyes and went back to sleep. There was nothing I can do until night time reached! It was Friday, 8:30P.M. I had just gotten out of the shower. I laid my black dress on the bed, sprayed a little of my Chanel perfume on the dress, and took out my fishnet stockings and black four-inch heels, along with my Diamond necklace and other Diamond Cartier watch. I poured two glasses of Remy Martin on the rocks, drank one glass quickly, and then, 10 minutes later, I drank another glass.

Watching time fly, I looked at the clock and it was now 8:50P.M. I walked in the bathroom, grabbed a pair of scissors, and cut off all of my hair, leaving nothing. The short cut gave me that rock star look. I put on my red fire lipstick, grey eye shadow, and penciled a dot up from my lip, giving me a mole. I slipped on my back dress and fishnet stockings, put my black sassy pumps on, grabbed my cell phone and grey clutch and black sunglasses, and strutted out of the room, waiting for Victoria to text me. After I closed the door, she text me to let me know that she was arriving at the hotel to give me the pictures. I waited for 15 minutes until she finally arrived, handing me a brown envelope. It was now 9:10P.M.

Victoria couldn't believe how different and sexy I looked. She couldn't stop staring at me. I walked toward the car and drove off. It took me 20 minutes to arrive at my house. When I drove passed to scope the scenery out, Bryant's car was parked in the driveway! He never has the alarm on when he's home. He always forgets, so I knew his every move. I knew he was upstairs in the room.

I parked the car around the corner from the house, grabbed the brown envelope, put it under my arm pit, and walked on the side if the house leading into the garage. I knew the side sensors were going to come on, so I waited until the lights cut off and then opened the side door. I walked toward the bookshelf to see if my acid was still there. It was. I grabbed the glass, tall gallon of acid, walked in the kitchen, grabbed a butcher knife, put it in my clutch purse, and tip-toed up the steps, leading toward the bedroom.

I heard the sound of music playing and candles lit. The bathroom door was closed and you could hear Bryant in the shower singing. I opened the bedroom door and the smell of Victoria Secret body spray was in the air. A red robe was laid out on the bed with rose petals on the bed and on the floor. I was enraged and so disappointed. I knew none of this was for me. Fucking candles burning and soft music, what was he thinking? I sat on the bed with my legs crossed until he got out of the shower. I set the acid on the side of the bed so he wouldn't see it. I wanted Bryant to confess. I wanted to scare him. As soon as the shower water cut off, Bryant stopped singing. I got up to turn the music down and he heard it. He opened the door and said, "Saniyah, is that you, baby? What are you doing here so soon?"

He opened the door and there I was, smiling. He didn't even notice who I was because my hair was cut completely off and I was so thin.

"Baby, let me explain," he said to me.

"Explain what, Bryant? You were waiting for Saniyah?" I asked him.

"No, why would you ask me that, Jocelyn?" he said, giving me a strange look. He closed the door slightly and said, "So, I guess you didn't go to Jamaica, huh?"

"I guessed I wasn't missed," I said to him, as the tears rolled down my face.

"What are you talking about now, Jocelyn?" he yelled.

"This!" I took the pictures out of the envelope and threw them in his face.

He looked at them and said, "Are you fucking crazy?"

I reached down in my clutch purse, grabbed the butcher knife and said, "Maybe I am," then walked toward him with my hands behind my back and began stabbing him in his chest-15 times in his heart and 10 times in his stomach, nonstop, until he fell to the ground, holding his chest. I watched him die slowly and looked at him suffer.

I then dragged his body from out of our bedroom into our bathroom and into the Jacuzzi tub; his body limbered and was very heavy. I picked his body up and put him in our Jacuzzi tub.

I walked into the room to try to hide the evidence. I opened the glass gallon of sulfuric acid and held my breath so I wouldn't inhale the fumes. I poured the whole gallon slowly on his face, and then his cock, then chest, watching his body sizzle and decompose. Tears ran down my face from the fumes that almost had me vomiting.

My mind went blank and my heart was racing. Once his body decomposed, I left out of the bathroom with no remorse and then slammed the door shut! I walked downstairs and sat on the couch. I just killed my husband and I didn't care. I felt relief from all of the stress he put me through.

I called the police and said to the dispatcher that I just killed my husband. Then, I hung the phone up. The police came 30 minutes later and put the handcuffs on me, got me up from the couch, and put me in the police car. The fumes were so strong that they were unable to walk in the bathroom to get him from out of the tub.

As I was walking out of the house, Saniyah was outside standing beside the police officers, crying and looking pitiful. Yellow caution tape was surrounding the house. I looked at her, smiled, and said loudly, "I win. You lose, bitch."

As the police put me in the back of the uncomfortable police car, I held my head down. I didn't even bother to look up. I must admit, I was satisfied. I smiled and then closed my eyes…

Jocelyn Carter was sentenced to life in prison, without parole, in the Federal Bureau of upstate New

Jersey. The jury found her guilty of first degree murder, on numerous accounts! Victoria Lanay Walker was never found. She didn't exist. When Detective Charles Mack and lawyers attempt to find her on the internet, she was not who she said she was. The person they found was deceased 20 years ago.

They then arrived at the lab where Victoria said she worked, but, once they arrived, the building was condemned. Jocelyn even attempted to call her several times on her cell phone, but the number was disconnected and was now untraceable. Victoria vanished after the night Bryant was murdered and the unmarked car was stolen without any evidence of fingerprints!

CPSIA information can be obtained at www.ICGtesting.com
Printed in the USA
LVOW08s2321041114

412001LV00011B/284/P